BORSTAL BOYS

Or simply : From Crime to Christ

By David Clarke

I have entitled this true story with the words of Aylesbury's Bucks Herald Newspaper headline, of 11th February 1971. This is because believers where first called Christians at Antioch by the world, so the title of my story has been adopted from the world of the media.

Published November 2013

Trojan Horse International
11 Hayling Close
Fareham Hampshire
PO14 3AE
E-mail : SecretaryDolores@yahoo.co.uk
Web Site: www.TrojanHorseInternational.com

ISBN: 97809539473-8-6 Printable Edition
ISBN: 97809539473-6-2 ePub Edition

1 Foreword Dr Philip Fleming

by Dr Philip Fleming MA. BA, Bch. FRCPsych. DPM

"Converted on LSD Trip"

This book, the personal testament of David Clarke, in an autobiographical style. It charts his life, which became one of criminality and drug taking though an experience in 1970 of finding God whilst under the influence of LSD. Cynics may say that this was just an effect of drugs, but it is clear that the experience changed his life. Later when in court facing charges he admitted to many other crimes and was fortunate in receiving three years conditional discharge and not a prison sentence.

Since then David has combined his work as a lecturer in electronics with his mission of spreading the word of God. This is a scrupulously honest book recording both the difficulties he has faced as well as the successes in his life since 1970. A continuing worry is the fat of his brother, currently serving a long prison sentence in a Philippine jail who himself has recently found God.

"This is an inspiring story of a life that has been turned from crime to a positive account and may be of help to others who find them selves directionless and involved in crime and drug misuse".

Dr. Philip M. Fleming. MA. BA, Bch. FRCPsych. DPM.

Consultant Psychiatrist with special responsibility for drugs and alcohol services. Kingsway House is the base for these services in Portsmouth.

2 Foreword Gregg Haslan

Rev Gregg Haslam Senior Minister Westminster Chapel London

Gregg Haslam

"David Clarke tells the story of his troubled violent past and his extraordinary life, in such a way that it re-tells the story of Jesus' love that's available for us all. Christ has the power to renew and reclaim anyone's wasted years, no matter we've done, or how deep our shame. He can re-launch our lives on a brand new future that we could never have planned for ourselves."

Westminster Chapel

London SW1E 6BS

3 Foreword Samuel Ntoyimondo

Chaplain HMPS Nottingham

" *This moving story demonstrates the goodness and mercy of God and it is a clear proof that no one is beyond God's grace, mercy and love. Whatever wrongdoings we do, God continues to call us back to Him and if we accept, He fulfils His plan for us to give us hope for the future.* "

Note from the author

Please excuse the typo's, errors in grammar and spelling. I was virtually illiterate until the age of 21 after which I learned to read and educate myself.

Please take time to understand what I am trying to communicate as to get proof readers to work for love is very difficult.

I am sure the New Testament writers, some of which were unlearned men, had the same difficulties.

Sincerely Yours

David Clarke

Contents

1	Foreword Dr Philip Fleming	3
2	Foreword Gregg Haslan	4
3	Foreword Samuel Ntoyimondo	5
4	What The Story Is About	17
5	About The Author	19
6	Confession To 24 crimes	22
	What To Do With Stolen Goods	23
	The Problem And A Cid Visit	23
	Testimony Of Barry Crown	25
	Testimony of Cyril Bryan	26
	Testimony of Mr E Connet	27
	I Speak In Court	27
	The Bucks Herald 11th February 1971	28
	Seeking Truth	29
	Voice Of Christ	30
	Difficulty	30
	My Story	32
7	My Early Life	32
	Sunday School	34

Roman Catholics Were Wrong	35
Lost and found	37
First Day At School	39
I Steal Money	41
Oldham My Home Town	41

8 Garston Infant School — 42

German Teacher	43
I Can't Read	43
David And The Hampster	44
Congregational Sunday School	45
What Was Easter All About ?	46
Cecil The Sissy And Air Pistol	47
I Get Electrocuted And Burned	48
Wrexham Holiday	49
The Fair At Garston, Paper Round And Stolen Bike	50
Don't Talk To Strangers	50
Playing Truant From School	51
Money Buys Many Things	51
Stolen Crystal Set	53
Stealing Radio Equipment	54
A Visit From The Police	54

Francis Coombe Secondary School	55
Michael and Boxing	55
My visit to Soho	56
Our Move To Wilstone	56
Keeping Myself Busy	57
I Ride A 350 cc Triumph	59
9 The Big Freeze 1962	**61**
Short Stay Back To Watford	62
My First Matchbox Radio	63
A Holiday in Newquay	63
Aylesbury: Our New Home	64
Bucks Herald News Article	65
I Steel Push Bikes	66
10 I Meet Mrs Grace Knight	**68**
Conversation Over The Intercom	69
Obituary Grace Maude Knight	70
A Confident 15 year old	71
11 Our Rock Group	**72**
Wild Willy Barrett	73
The Fowler Mean our Rock group	73
A Secret	74

Playing At Courts Dance School	76
Oxford Bags	81
My First Girl Friend	81
Love is Strange	82
Carknapping	83
Sniffing Chloroform	83
Banbury Gaff	84
The Great Train Robbery	85
The Kray Twins	86
Kray's Imprisonment	87
Reputation Was Important	87
Mods, Rockers, Scooters, Bikes a Bubble Car	87
Pete Townsend Gives Us A Lift	88
The Bubble Car	89
Dr Clarke's Case	90
Adventures In The Bubble Car	91
Having a Crack	92
Off to Margate Bank Holiday	92
Webley air gun and the Bubble Car	92
Caught by the Police	93
All Coppers Are Bastards	93
Bubble Car Blows Up	94

I Get The Sack	95
Plan A Break In	95

12 Canterbury Prison — 96

Canterbury Prison Together	97
All Screws Were Bastards	97
Canterbury Prison	98
Porridge For Breakfast	99
Moved to Different Cells	100
Hair Style Change	101
What Sentence Have You Got?	102
Wormwood Scrubs	102
Dover Borstal (The Citadel)	102
News Via The Grape Vine	103
How To Deal With Bullying	103
Electrical Installation Course	106
Paternity Suite	106

13 My Release From Borstal — 107

Home Leave From Borstal	108
Returning to Aylesbury	108
A Suit Made	109
Government Training Centre Enfield	109
I Build A 4 Valve Superhet Radio	110

Seventh Day Adventist	110
I Visit Michael In Maidstone Prison	110
Escape From Prison	111
Smuggling Gold	111
I Am Not Me I'm My Brother	112
Chloroform and its Effects	113
Mods, Skinheads, Greasers at Yarmouth	113
Newquay Here We Come	115
The Beatles Magical Mystery Tour	115
Our Holiday to Newquay the place of the Sun	117
I Am A Waiter at the Gull Rock Hotel	117
We Return Home to Aylesbury	118
A Marriage In Gretna Green	118
Our Trip to Shoreham	119
The History of the Jews and 1967	119
Pat Jones And The Bully	120

14 Conversion from Crime to Christ — 121

A Bad LSD Trip	121
Dave I Am With You	127
All I Could Do Was Tell Them	127
Why Boast	128

15 What after Salvation — 129

- Evidence of the New birth — 129
- What to do with Stolen Goods — 130
- I Seek To Tell Others — 131
- My Own Ignorance, I Never Read The Bible — 132
- Difference at College — 132
- I Tell Rupert — 133
- Turning From The World — 133
- Religious And None Religious Persons — 134
- Being Kept By The Power And Grace Of God — 134
- What To Do With Stolen Goods — 135
- My Citroen DS Car — 135
- A Stolen Mini 1968 — 136
- Returning The Trolley Jack — 137
- Dealing With Sin And Temptation — 138
- On The Love of God — 138
- Hippies in the Shed — 139
- Using The Stolen Shed at Mount Street — 139

16 Going to Church — 140

- Not Dressed For An Occasion — 140
- I Attend Various Churches — 141
- Giving A Testimony — 143

I Am Baptized ... 143
Mormons and Baptism ... 145
Baptism in the Spirit ... 146
The Christian Life ... 146
The Divine Nature Of Jesus Christ ... 147
Preaching Or Musical Entertainment ... 147
Giving my Testimony ... 148
Every Day the Sabbath Day ... 148
Authorized Version of the Bible ... 148
Giving Money ... 149
Sunday Cloths And Judging By Appearance ... 150
Doing The Work Of An Evangelist ... 150
I Meet Peter Howe Minister Of The Gospel ... 152
I Was Told I Was A Hyper-Calvinist ... 152
Doctrinal Summery ... 152
I Hear Dr Martin Lloyd Jones Preach ... 153

17 Getting a Job ... 154
Acting Foolishly ... 155
Working For Self ... 155
Delivered From Fire, The Morgan Sports Car ... 156
I Find Work In Lowestoft ... 157
Elim Pentecostal ... 157

Working For Mr C J Ward And Son	159
My Theological Training Dr John Gill	159
Michael Goes To Spain	159
My Visit To Spain	160
Pentecostal Holiness Church	160
Do Not Be led By feelings	162
Opposition To Imputed Righteouness	162
I Leave The Pentecostal Holiness Church	163
The Three Day Week And My Redundancy	163
My Redundancy	164
My reference	164
My Response To Redundancy	165

18 Working for Granada T.V. Rentals — 165

My Visit To Northern Ireland	166
Meeting Dr Ian Paisley	168
Suspicious Looking Suit Case	168
The Wrong Part of Belfast	168
We Go To The Reformation Conference	170

19 Mr Victor Prince — 171

20 Bierton Particular Baptists — 173

Distinguishing Doctrines of Grace	173
Bierton Particular Baptists Articles of Religion	175

Denham's Hymns	175
The Doctrines Of The Gospel	176
This Jesus Had Called Me	177
Not all Preaching Was Good	177
Miss Ruth Ellis	177
Miss Bertha Ellis	178
My wife joins the Church at Bierton	178
Hats Or Head Coverings For Ladies	178

21 A Call to Preach the Gospel — 180

I Did Not Believe In Bible Colleges	181
Wolverhampton Polytechnic And Teacher Training	181
An Ulterior Motive	181
I Inform The Church Of My Felt Call To Preach	182
Questioned About The Law Of Moses	182
Mr Hill's Conclusion	183
The Papal visit 1982	183
A Spanking from the pulpit	185
Preaching The Gospel	187

22 I Go Fishing For Men — 189

Bierton Meeting 5th June 1983	190
Meeting Televised	190
A News Paper Report	190

4 What The Story Is About

This is a true story of two brothers, Michael John Clarke (1946), and David Clarke (1949), who were born in Oldham, Lancashire, England.

The story portrays a remarkable change that took place, in the life of David when he was 20 years old, on the night of the 16th January 1970. His brother Michael was left untouched.

These brothers influenced each other during, the 50's & 60's, and resulted in both David and Michael serving time in prison. David was sent to Dover Borstal, and Michael Maidstone Prison, for charges of malicious wounding, and carrying a firearm without a licence.

The story speaks in detail, of all the significant events in David's life, from being a child through to the time of his conversion to Christ, and then recounts the consequent difficulties that he experienced, as he tried to follow the way of Christ. This led David to make a confession to the Police about his 24 crimes, and the recovery of much stolen property. The story appeared as news headlines in the Bucks Herald on 11th February, 1971 and led to a remarkable conditional discharge. It was believed, by many of Aylesbury's criminal world, that Dave had gone mad after taking LSD, or the story was an ingenious plan devise by David to prevent him from being sent to prison again, for crimes against society. This was not the case as the story will tell.

Michael continued his life in the direction he was going and married. He had a daughter and a brief flamboyant life-style in business. He became the company Managing Director of *Tudor Charm*, a manufacturing company in Milton Keynes and enjoyed the success of business for a season. This eventually came to an end by his company going into liquidation, and him into deep depression, leading to his broken marriage and divorce. Michael sought to restart in business, after his divorce, and moved to Thailand, starting his company called *Paradise Movies*, which led to his further troubles, and reports of various scams, in Thailand, that were published in the News of the World, in 1992.

Finally he took the ideas that he had learned in Patiya, Bangkok, to the Philippines, and commenced his Travel Agency, called, *Paradise Express* selling holidays, whose main attractions were, Adult Pleasures for men only. This hit international news, and led to a criminal conviction. He was condemned to serve a 16-year prison sentence, in New Bilibid Prison, in 1996. Michael always maintained his innocence.

When this story was first written Michael was a broken man, in body and in health. He had no hope for the future.

It was during this time that Michael had contacted David and told him of his despair, and his friendship with Sunny Wilson who had been sentenced to death in the Philippines, in 1996. When the Supreme Court, acquitted Sunny, on 19th December 1999, he gave Michael a paperback book, which was C.S. Lewis's, *Mere Christianity.* It was this book, which convinced Michael that Jesus was the Christ and led to his baptism in the prison. David, believed God was able to save Michael and give him hope for the future, even though he had lived a life far from God in the past, and was now serving a near life-sentence, in an awful third world prison.

The story is real, remarkable, and demonstrates the goodness and mercy of God, in saving one through Jesus Christ, and the severity of God in leaving another to himself. But now, it is as though Michael too had been plucked, like a brand from the burning fire.

David now believes that both he, and Michael although criminals in the 60's, were victims of Manic Depression, and they have both suffered from hypo-manic episodes. However their belief systems conditioned the way that they reacted to their mood swings, and may well account for some of their remarkable experiences that are recorded in this book.

This story could be of real help to Judges, Magistrates, psychiatrists, psychiatric nurses, doctors, social workers, solicitors, policemen, ministers of religion, lecturers, teachers and probation officers. Also it could be helpful to Christians and those who suffer from manic depression or dyslexia. It could also be a means of help to reform criminals, and useful to those living in the margins of society, along with unruly youths, drug users, and hardened criminals. It could also be a help to any one contemplating, or going through divorce.

David Clarke   *David Clarke*

Michael John Clarke   *michael Clarke*

5 About The Author

David Clarke was a lecturer at Fareham College, in Hampshire, England, when he first published the first edition of this book, on the 11th of February 2001. It was there that he taught Electronic Servicing, from September 1989 through to August, 2001.

He was educated and trained to be a lecturer, at Wolverhampton Polytechnic, and graduated with a Certificate in Education, which was awarded by Birmingham University, in 1978. He commenced teaching at Luton College of Higher Education that year, and has taught hundreds of students during his 21 years as a lecturer.

David has six children, the oldest of which is Isaac John Clarke who won the title of King of Southsea, in 2011, as he was the BMX champion, in Portsmouth, for that year. His other children are Esther Jane Clarke, Eleanor Mary Clarke, David Martin Luther Clarke, Rebekah Alice Clarke and Maisie Layla Clarke.

However David's earlier life had been rather different, and since leaving Dover Borstal, which was a young persons prison, in 1968, he had a 3-year career of undetected crime, until the night of the 16th of January, 1970, when he experienced a Christian conversion, whilst suffering from the effects of LSD.

David was not the only person of his generation to have a religious experience. Many famous pop stars, celebrities and sports people have had religious experiences. Cliff Richards, Paul Jones, the lead singer in Manfred Mann, Helen Shapiro, the 60's pops stars all became Christians. So did George Foreman the famous boxer, Regie Kray the famous gangster. George Harrison of the Beatles and Pete Townsend of The Who all has some form of religious experience. Also many later pops stars, like Katie Perry, Alice Cooper, all had a Christian religious experience.

Both he and his older brother Michael were both convicted criminals in the 60's, and had served time in prison, for charges of malicious wounding, and carrying a fire arm without a license.

On the night of the 16th of January 1970, their life paths turned in different directions and the next fourteen years, David read and studied the scriptures, leading him to join the Bierton, Strict and Particular Baptist Church in 1976, and was ordained as a Strict Baptist minister, in 1983.

David married in 1977 and had four children, two of which were twins. In June 1984 David held a special meting at the Bierton Strict and Particular Baptist Church where he told his story of conversion from crime the Christ to many of his friends who came to that meeting.

It was after this that David's troubles appeared to begin and he felt compelled to resign from the Bierton Church, after which he wrote his first book, *The Bierton Crisis*, that explained his reason for his secession.

Michael mean while, found himself in trouble and was sentenced to prison in the Philippines, in 1996. This led David to go on a mission, to the Far East, in 2001 with a friend Gordon Smith, in order to bring relief and help to Michael. Michael too had turned from Crime to Christ and help share his testimony to hundreds of criminals in the largest prison in Asia's Far East.

It was then David believed that it was time to complete his student's education, and wrote his second book, ***Converted on LSD Trip.***

Since then he has spoken to many of his friends of all what Jesus has done for him. He wished to make known to all his students and friends that his bad experience on LSD, was nothing compared to the experience of Hell.

Like Oscar Schindler, and his list, all that were on that list were saved, who otherwise would have perished at the hands of the Nazi's. So too, this David had a list of over 250 students and friends, that he wanted to contact. He wished to persuade them to listen, and hear in full; of all what Jesus Christ had done for him and what he could do for others. David now wishes to reach a wider audience.

David met Dave Courtney in 2004, and he promised to help David tell his story to help others , think again and may be turn from crime and avoid a criminal record.

Sadly Michael died in the prison in May 2005, from tuberculosis, before their vision of bringing help to many was realised, in May 2005. And now David wishes to bring a message of hope to all his friends. David believed that at the first publication of his book he had a word of encouragement from the Lord about his testimony, which is this:

"And he was astonished, and all that were with him, at the draught of fishes which they had taken: Luke 5 verse 9."

6 Confession To 24 crimes

It was real, absolutely real, but none of my friends really believed me. All I could do was tell them what had happened to me, and that was what I did. I told them all, the long, the short and the tall. As many of them as I could. They thought I had gone mad after taking LSD.

Jesus Christ had spoken to me and rescued me from a bad LSD trip on Friday evening, 16th January 1970. He had said that what I had been going through was nothing compared to what hell was like. I now knew the way and was determined to tell the others. I had become a Christian and no longer needed to live the life style that I had adopted, which had involved crime, drugs, promiscuity, flash cars and fame. I had been born again.

I was now responsible for sorting out all my stolen gear. What could be done with a builder's shed and stolen cars? I still had in my possession many stolen goods, which included the 48-foot by 24-foot builders shed, which we had stolen one night from a building site at Berkhampstead, and a lovely "G" reg. Mini, stolen from Hemel Hempstead, which was in the process of being rung. Ringing meant replacing the new stolen mini with legitimate registration documents and number plates from an older scrape car. My new mini was being used to replace it. This was to be my new car. I also had a Morris Minor Traveller, which had been "rung" and was being used as a hire car. I had stolen garage equipment, which included an air compressor, electric welding equipment, spray guns and a trolley jack. I also had several pieces of electrical test equipment, which included oscilloscopes, AVO meters and Colour T.V.'s. I had all the garage equipment that I needed to repair and spray cars.

I had a lovely Citroen DS car in the builder's shed, which was being repaired. I obtained this car through swapping it for a colour T.V. set. The only problem was that I had stolen the T.V. set from an old people's at Redfields old peoples home in Winslow, Buckinghamshire.

I also had two nice speedboat engines, getting ready for the summer of 1970. All in all I had a real good time full of excitement and fun.

In fact I had been stopped in the midst of my career, which involved stealing all kinds of goods to have a good time. I had intended to have a caravan, a speedboat, water skis, aqualung diving gear, flash cars, motorbikes, and clothes and so on, all through stealing. I was in fact stopped whilst in the midst of my career but not by the police. It was Jesus Christ who had called me by name and I followed him.

What To Do With Stolen Goods

I thank God he intervened again a year later and His hand was clearly seen once more. I had no one else to help. As I write this I take encouragement in the faithfulness of God to me, in never leaving me or forsaking me. I realize now I was kept through the power and grace of our Lord Jesus Christ to bare witness today, to many people of the goodness and mercy of God.

The Problem And A Cid Visit

I was sitting at the table in our kitchen at 37 Finmere Crescent one evening in late 1971, when a knock came on the door. I had two visitors, a detective constable Robson and a younger man. I was greeted quite politely but with sure and certain words, You are charged with stealing a colour television set, and would you accompany us down to the police station to make a statement ?

I knew instantly what I must do and say. I saw the hand of God and believed this was all his doing but I did not know the outcome. Leaving the outcome to God I asked the two men to sit down in the kitchen and I admitted the charge. At this D.C. Robson seemed most relieved, for he said to me later, he had thought I would be very difficult and awkward and deny the charge.

I explained I would certainly come with them to the police station and make a statement but I wanted to speak to them about other things first. I said I had many crimes that I wished to tell them about but wanted to tell them first of all why I was informing them.

I wanted it to be known that they would not have been able to find out about my crimes unless I confessed to them and I wanted to testify to the saving work of Jesus Christ that he had saved me from my former criminal way of life a year previously and that I did not wish to get off lightly with this confession but rather bear testimony for Christ. For in no way could my crimes be discovered unless I tell them and owned up to them. I had a lot of property, which could be returned.

I went with them to the police station and spent the rest of the evening making written statements giving details of my crimes. I was detained that evening in the police cells at Walton Street police station in Aylesbury, not that I was a stranger to prison cells as I will tell later. My shoelaces were removed but I was allowed my New Testament (Authorized Version, working mans pocket addition).

I had to appear in Aylesbury's Magistrates Court on the 9th February 1971 and answered two charges of burglary and one of theft. I also asked for 21 other crimes of theft to be taken into consideration, all of which had been committed since I left Borstal, between September 1967 and 16th January 1970. I had decided I did not need legal representation, as I would speak for my self.

With my past record of probation and Borstal training it was quite expected that I would be sent to prison. I was quite OK with this because I deserved it, and I believed God was in this, and had a definite purpose in this event. I prepared for this by setting my affairs in order at home and gave directions that my Mini Traveller, which I had rebuilt, was to be given to Barry Crown, if I got sent down. I believed that whatever happened to me the outcome was of God and there would be good reason for it. I thought I might be being sent to prison so as to preach the gospel to inmates. A friend of mine Mr Peter Murray was concerned about my court appearance and suggested I get some written testimonials from some of my Christian friends and he felt he ought to appear in person and speak on my behalf. The friends who wrote were Barry Crown, Cyril Bryan, Tom Thompson and Eric Connet. I am including these letters, which were sent to the court. These people all testify to the saving grace of God in changing my life. These are some of the written testimonies:

Testimony Of Barry Crown

R.B. Crown 45, Mitcham Walk, Aylesbury. Buckinghamshire.

To the Clerk to the Magistrates

Dear Sir,

6th February 1970

I am a graduate of Salford University, and hold a B. Sc. In Civil Engineering. I am at present an employee of Aylesbury Borough Council, working under Mr. Hanney, the Borough Engineer and Surveyor. I have held this post since September 1970.

Shortly after taking up residence in Aylesbury I befriended Mr. David Clarke whom I met at the Full Gospel Church, Rickford's Hill. I found David to be a true and sincere Christian seeking to spread the Gospel of Jesus Christ and to give personal testimony of the salvation through Jesus Christ, which he himself had experienced.

David told me how he had been miraculously converted on January 16th 1970. And was the reason for the subsequent change in his whole manner and outlook to life. Before his conversion he confessed to a life of drugs and theft, but now he no longer had any desire or pleasure in such things, since Christ destroyed the power of such in his life.

For the six months I have known David I have been a witness to the truth of his testimony and I know him as a person who is a completely honest and trustworthy follower of the Christian faith.

Yours Sincerely,

R. B. Crown.

Testimony of Cyril Bryan

176 Cambridge Street Aylesbury

To the Clerk to the Magistrates

2/2/71

Dear Sir,

I am privileged to write a testimony to you concerning David Clarke, and I count it a privilege because it is to the glory of God.

I have known this young man through conversations and meeting with him, through the church I attend in Aylesbury. The Full Gospel Testimony Church at Rickford's Hill.

What I wish to bring to your notice is the wonderful change that has taken place in him as a result of him believing the gospel and receiving the Lord Jesus Christ as his personal saviour, according to the scriptural instruction and ordinances.

The change of character and speech is miraculous, as are all the works of God, and as a believer in the Lord Jesus Christ for 30 years; I know that David Clarke is a transformed person, by the grace of God. As are we all who know the reality of the new birth as taught by Johns Gospel.

You will know his past life, I testify to his new life in Christ

Jesus. Yours Sincerely,

C Bryan.

Testimony of Mr E Connet

E.H. Connet

125 Park Street,

Aylesbury,

TO WHOM IT MAY CONCERN

2nd February 1971

This is to certify that I have known Mr. Clarke for a period of approximately 9 months since his conversion to Christianity. I am fully persuaded that he has turned his back on his past life and changed for the better.

He is now earnestly endeavoring to make amends for his past mistakes and even influence others to turn their lives over to God, as he has done.

My object in writing this testimonial is that it may help to throw some light on David's character from one who knows him as a Christian.

Yours Faithfully,

E Connet.

I Speak In Court

I appeared in court on the 9th February 1971, dressed in my dark blue (Mod) suit. I pleaded guilty and then a report from the police was read and I was given leave to speak for myself. I spoke extempore (without notes- trusting in the Lord for all the help I needed) describing my pre- conversion days up to my conversion. I also spoke about life since being a Christian explaining my difficulties with respect to the stolen goods that I had in my possession.

I was able to speak of what Jesus had done for me in a way that only God could have worked.

After this Peter Murray spoke on my behalf confirming my testimony.

This happened on Tuesday 9th February 1971, a date that proved significant to me 3 years later.

I was amazed, so were all my Christian friends. The magistrates thought I was trying to be a martyr. I do not know how or why. They obviously thought I should be sent to prison but part of my punishment would be that I was not going to get what I wanted. God smiled. We smiled with him. It was good to be a child of God.

The whole court appearance was reported in the local newspapers and in the national Evening Standard.

The news headlines of the Bucks Herald read, Why he confessed to 24 crimes and Converted on LSD trip. Whilst the Bucks Advertiser read Man speaks of horrors on LSD".

The above is a copy of those headlines, all of which were fairly accurate.

The Bucks Herald 11th February 1971

Reads as follows; David Clarke, who had a three-year career of undetected crime, experienced a "Christian conversion" whilst suffering from the effects of LSD, he told Aylesbury magistrates, on Tuesday. After wrestling with his conscience for a year, he confessed to 24 crimes, and gave information leading to the recovery of over £1000 worth of stolen property. In court he pleaded guilty to charges of steeling a £300 colour television set from an old peoples home, a £20 spray gun, and a hydraulic jack.

News Head lines

The Bucks Herald Weekly Paper

Head Line news Bucks Herald (Click to view)

He asked for 21 other charges to be taken into consideration, including stealing a builders shed, two cars, and an electric arc welder, two other T.V. sets, two compressors, and a road trailer. Clarke (21) of Finmere Crescent said that his reputation in the town had been that of a man who was enjoying himself. I used to sell drugs to young people, and indulge in permissive sex, he declared.

Seeking Truth

Religion to me was rubbish, and for sissy people who could not stand on their own feet, he said. "Within my heart I was searching for truth, and a meaning to life". He had good prospects of getting on in life he went on but was not satisfied with what I had, I was greedy, selfish and boastful. Clarke had been using pep pills, and marijuana since he was 16 he told the court, but it was after taking LSD that he experienced, what he described as, a major thing in my life. He described the torment he suffered, as a result of taking the drug, and went on I warn any young person who hears my testimony, The effects of LSD are so bad, and I warn you to stay clear. While in this condition he said he, called on the name of Jesus and his torment went from him.

Voice Of Christ

Jesus Christ spoke to me as clearly as I speak here today saying, David, I am with you.

Mr Murray, of Manor Crescent, Wendover said he was habitually sceptical of sudden conversions, and preferred to put them to the test of time. The time, which had elapsed, since Clarke's profession of faith had convinced him that this young man would now be salt and light to society". He is in truth, a new man, and had experienced what Christ called a second birth. Murray said Clarke now put himself out to be of assistance, read the bible intensely, always carried a New Testament, attended a wide circle of churches and would spend hours in discussion on spiritual things.

Difficulty

Clarke's difficulty during the months spent deciding how to make amends for his past had been the problem of accusing himself, without informing on others.

Passing sentence the chairman of the magistrates, Colonel I. Tetley, told Clarke, You have pleaded guilty to three offenses and asked us to take into consideration 21 others, and except a record over a short period of time, which is quite the worst we have ever seen, we have considered what we aught to do and have come to the conclusion that your evident desire to become a martyr is one we are not going to gratify.

He gave Clarke a conditional discharge for three years pointing out that the sincerity of his conversion could be shown by his behaviour during that period.

The outcome of the court case was a complete surprise to us all, and we were overjoyed. A Christian friend, Mrs. Chapski of Broughton Avenue, Aylesbury, invited us all back to her home for coffee.

D.C. Robson informed me that they had discovered I was the person who had stolen the television from Mike West. An enemy of Mike West had tipped them off about the stolen television. Mike West appeared in Court on the same day as myself and was fined £25. He nearly lost his job with the insurance company that he worked for. His encounter at court, to his embarrassment, also appeared on the front page of the newspaper alongside the article about my conversion.

After this I gave Mike West his Citroen car back that I had swapped for the colour T.V.. I had re sprayed it a bright Banana yellow, and replaced the engine. At lease he was able to sell it and get some money back. I now know, and take encouragement that God works well and sorts things out when we cannot do so.

As far as the other stolen goods were concerned the police managed to take away most of them but the firm who owned the builders shed sent a trailer. The ironic thing is that I could get no help to load the shed on the trailer. In the end Mrs. Knight was the only one to help. This was very hard work but between us we managed to load it on the trailer late one night. To give you some idea of the value of the stolen items. The shed was said to be worth £400. The mini was brand new and worth £672. The price of a terraced house at that time was £2000.

My Story

I wish to tell my story starting when I was born (natural birth) and lead the reader until my conversion when the Lord Jesus spoke to me (second birth).

I then wish to speak about being a Christian and seeking to follow the Lord and meeting with the many and varied Christian groups and people. I wish to share with the reader how I learned the distinctive truths of the doctrines of grace and the sovereignty of God, which led me to joining the Bierton Strict and Particular Baptist Church.

In this account I relate my call to preach and I list the many churches I share the gospel with until the very sad occasion of my secession from the Bierton Church due to a departure for the truth. The church fell into the error of allowing general redemption being taught and a falling away into the error of the Law of Moses becoming their rule of life and conduct, rather than the Gospel. My secession being fully recorded on my publication, **The Bierton Crisis,** which I now believe could serve as a real help to many churches, as in this account I name the many errors that I found to be prevalent in those days amongst believers, and I point out the truth and scriptural view, which opposed those who held had fallen into error.

It is my desire that this will serve to help and edify fellow Christians, and those seeking the truth as it is in Jesus Christ.

7 My Early Life

I was born on the 16th February 1949 at 9.50 AM, in Boundary Park General hospital, Oldham, Lancashire. My mother's name was Elsie Dyson Clarke who was married to my father Thomas George Clarke some time after the war. She informed me that this hospital was next to Oldham Athletic football ground.

We lived with my mother's father in his house at 26 Fleet Street, Clarksfield, Oldham. My granddad's name was Watts Ormrod and he was a retired craftsman and senior member of a Trades Union. His hair was white, which I am told happened due to an accident at work when a large rivet was pushed through his hand.

Boundary Park Hospital

This Is Where I Was Born

I had a brother, who was two and a half years older than me, Michael John (spelt Michael instead of Michael due to my mother's stubbornness when he was named at the registrar's office. The official informed her that the way she had spelt Michael was in fact wrong, and my mum reacted at being corrected and insisted it would be spelt just as she had written it.

My mum and dad were both in the armed forces and were very proud to be British. Dad was in the Army and mum was in the Royal Air Force.

I was christened at Christ's Church, Glodwick and my Godfather was David Maltby of 382 Barton Road; Stratford and was a sides man at the Church on Barton Road. He gave me at that time a bible with a text of scripture written on the inside cover.

My Parents

Thomas George Clarke   **Elsie Dyson Clarke**

Prov. 3. 6 "In all thy ways acknowledge him and he shall direct thy paths ". I have found a baptism certificate dated 3rd April 1949, where it states I became a member of Christ the child of God, and an inheritor of the "Kingdom of Heaven". This however is wrong, as I did not become a member of Christ until I was born again on The 16th January 1970, which I speak about later.

My Baptismal Certificate

David's Baptismal Certificate 3rd April 1949

Sunday School

I remember attending the church and Sunday school at Christ Church, which was just along the road from our house in Fleet Street. On one occasion I was so cosy, sitting on the pew, I fell asleep and woke up with a jolt wondering where I was, just as the vicar had finished his sermon. I had been lulled into sleep by the stimulating sermon. I haven't changed even to day. I must have been about 3 or 4 years old. It was my mother's idea to take my brother and I to Sunday school.

Barnabus Sunday School

Barnabus Sunday School Building

At Sunday school I remember we painted pictures of houses and still remember wondering why did the teacher draw the house with the door in the middle of the building and windows either side of the door. This was because I knew we lived in a house in a terrace and our door was to one side, just like the other houses in the street. I had no spiritual impressions of the Lord Jesus Christ from these times.

Roman Catholics Were Wrong

Just across the street from our house there was a great Roman

Catholic Church building, and living accommodation, surrounded by a high wall. It was built of red engineering bricks and several stories high with stained glass windows alone the long church building. I remember looking up at the crooked lightening conductor and I still get the feeling of austerity and awkwardness when wondering what was behind that wall. It produced the same feeling in me when I had the story of Toby Twirl red to me. In that story he meets a giant who lived behind a great high walled castle. I was afraid to go near, or to even think of climbing the wall, or trespass in the grounds. I did not know it was a Roman Catholic Church building until about 25 years later when my mother informed me.

Roman Catholic Building

The Roman Catholic Building

At that time I knew of no other religion than that of the Church of England, I assumed my mother was right in all such matters and so the Catholics were wrong.

I remember the street lamps because a man use to come around each night to light them as they were gas and he had a small ladder, which he carried with him, pointed at one end. He climbed the ladder and lit the lamps each night. I assume they were gas lamps.

I remember my favourite sweets were what was called Kylie, it is called sherbet now. We could also buy a very small loaf of bread called a penny loaf.

The Back Of Our House

Back Yard of 26 Fleet Street

Lost and found

At that time when I was about 4 years old I wanted to go to another Sunday School (I did not know at the time it was at a church building), which was at Lee's Road. My mother must have taken me there before. On this occasion it was Saturday morning and I did not believe there was no Sunday School that day. After being dressed I think my mother must have humoured me and did not take me seriously. I said I was going to Sunday School. I left home, I do not think my Mum realized and I walked at least two miles along Balfor Street and along the busy Lee's Road and found the building. To my disappointment it was all locked up. On my return I wandered off and got lost and ended up asking for help from a Laundry Shop. They put me in the window as a lost boy and called the police. I was soon returned home. I think my Mum was horrified how far I had been.

Back Alley

Back Alley at 26 Fleet Street

I commenced my school days at "Clark's Field" infants' school. My brother Michael John was already attending and was in the third year when I started.

Clark's Field Infants School

(David's 1st Class, David Bottom Right)

First Day At School

I remember my first day at school in the classroom with other children. The ceilings were high and there were things like sand pits, black board easels, old fashion classroom desks and tables.

The girl next door, Vivian Butler, began school with me and I can remember her crying for her Mum. I remember not feeling the need to cry and I tried to comfort her and assure her all would be well.

My Auntie Edith was very good to us boys and we would visit her every Saturday. She lived with my Granddad's sister. She was called Auntie Alice. Auntie Edith would take us out to a great park in Oldham and on the way home we would call in at the chip shop. In those days chips were real chips, cooked in real fat. One of our favourite meals she would cook was potato pie, with red cabbage. In the house there was a cellar, which I always liked to visit. I think at one time washing was done in the cellar.

Michael's Class Clark's Field Infants

Michael Bottom Centre

At that time my brother was probably the only close friend I had, although we were not too close. He was just there.

We use to go swimming on a Saturday morning to the "Waterhead Baths". This type of swimming baths was typical of the old-fashioned baths of the time. They were small, the water green, and walls tiled cream. At the side of the pool there were slipper baths where you could sit up to your chin in hot water and carbolic soap was supplied to wash with. It was very cosy. In fact the whole atmosphere was warm and cosy, not like the cold clinical swimming baths of modern times. Next-door was the wash house where mum used to go at the same time to do washing.

One Saturday morning I nearly drowned and was saved by the attendant called Norman. I had tiptoed backwards and as the pool got slowly deeper and deeper I found I could not touch the bottom. It was through the providence of God that the attendant turned to see me reaching upwards out of the water. I couldn't speak. He dived in to rescued me and I can still feel the fear today of nearly drowning.

Across the road from the swimming baths was a slaughterhouse, next door to inhabited houses. We were very curious and would look through the slatted windows and see the men kill the pigs, sheep and cattle. This was awesome and ghoulish and a fearful thing, but we were very curious and wanted to see how the men slew the animals. There was blood, animal intestines, animal heads bones and blood. The smell was awful and not pleasant at all, and it seemed as though the pigs knew they were going to be slaughtered, and their end was come.

I have wondered about my brother since then, as he was two and a half years older than me and how this may have affected him. Later on in life he demonstrated a callous way, which was characteristic of killing without mercy just like these slaughter men.

About this time I remember coming home from school and in the dusk of that day the house seemed unusually quiet. I noticed some blood on my brother's book and my mum told me there had been an accident. My brother had fallen down a basement stairway shaft at school and landed on his back. He was concussed and I remember then feeling how precious life was. My brother could have died through the fall. It was awesome. I still had no recollection of God during this time.

I Steal Money

On one occasion my parents were invited to their friends for the day. They owned a pub and had two boys both younger than me. On this occasion I was on my own and I noticed that the till in the pub was open, and money was available. I quickly took some money and walked out of the room. In order to cover up my tracks I went and told the parents of the boys that they had pressed the till button and the till had opened. That was a lie made up to cover up my sin and I tried to pass the blame onto their children. I felt bad after that, and still do, as not only had I taken their money but it would also put my parents into disrespect, having a thief as a son.

Oldham My Home Town

Oldham is a town in the north of England, not far from the city of Manchester, and during the 19th century was an industrial community famous for its cotton mills. In fact, my grandfather was a great supporter of the Trades Union.

As a child I remember the old mills, red brick built with huge chimneys towering high above the buildings. Also the water reservoirs, which we were always warned to stay away from. My mother had spoken about children being drowned in them and this was sufficient for me to obey her.

An Oldham Mill

Old Mill in Oldham Lancashire England

8 Garston Infant School

We moved from Oldham to Garston, Watford when I was 5 years old and my mum took me to my first day at school, which was at Garston Infant School. I was in the second year of the infants. My mum had arranged for me to walk home with a girl called Vivian who apparently lived in Coats Way where we lived. Not that I knew my address because I didn't. All I knew was we had move to a place called Garston, so I assumed we lived in Garston Road.

When it came to walking home I had to follow Vivian, but she took me by a way I had never been before. A completely different way, and across a park to what was the other end of Coats Way. She left me there and I had no Idea where I was, as I did not recognize anywhere at all. Feeling uneasy about all this I realized I was lost. So I made my way back towards the school and began to ask people where Garston Road was. There was no such place but I insisted I lived in Garston Road. A man with a red Bedford dormobile offered to take me back to school to find out where I lived so off we went. The schoolteacher said I lived in Coats Way where Vivian had took me but I said I didn't live there, as I could not recognize the place. The man took me back to Coats Way but I could not recognize where I lived. He drove from one end to the other. It was quite a long Way with a council estate on one end and private houses at the other end. This was where I lived, 149 Coats Way. I saw my Mum in the front garden so I arrived home after being lost on my first day at school.

German Teacher

My classroom teacher was a German woman called Miss Kitchinger. She spoke with a German accent and I spoke with a broad Lancashire accent. We did not hit it off and I was hopeless at reading the flash cards. It seemed as though I was singled out and proved to be a dunce, as I could not really read. Being small I messed about to divert attention from my inability to do class work.

One day when I arrived at school I found a pair of pumps on my desk (they called them plimsolls now), which I later found out belonged to Vivian and I did not like them being there. Feeling rather indignant I place them in the dustbin. I think I might have asked the teacher, "please Miss, whose are these pumps?", But I was ignored, as she did not understand me, so in the bin they went.

The next day Vivian's mother came to school wanting to find out where her plimsolls had gone. The caretaker said he had found them and placed them on my desk. When I was questioned I was in trouble and Miss Kitchinger said my mum would have to buy a new pair as I had thrown them away. I felt this unfair and felt really picked on. I know my mum came to the school and had an argument about the pumps and the fact that a German teacher was trying to teach English. This was only few years after the war with Germany had ended.

I Can't Read

I realised I could not read at the age of 6 years old and this difficulty showed it self in class when we had to read flash cards. When it was my turn I just could not tell what was written and I felt embarrassed. It was humiliating. As a result I felt the need to distract the attention from any action that involved me reading and cause a disturbance of some kind. I was known as a naughty boy. And to top it all, the kids mocked my northern accent.

David And The Hampster

At that time my mum had to work late and it was arranged for me to wait in the classroom after school until my mum came to pick me up. This was shortly after the event with the plimsolls. The class had a pet hamster and this little creature got all the attention from every one. I was the one that got no attention but rather got into trouble. One evening whilst I was waiting in the classroom for my mum to collect me, the teacher left the classroom for a short while.

I went towards the hamster cage and thought to my self why do you get all the attention. I know what I am going to do with you. I took the hamster out to the cage and closed the door. I looked at the hamster in the eyes and went over to Vivian's desk and put it inside, shutting the lid quickly thinking that will pay her back for getting me in trouble over her plimsolls. I sat back in my chair before the teacher returned and went home with my mum as though nothing had happened.

The next day I went into class as quiet as I could and keeping out of the way. I waited patiently for the eruptions. Then suddenly, Oh Miss, screamed Vivian, the hamster is in my desk. It had weeded and messed everywhere through out the night. Every one gathered around the desk to see at the same time. I felt very guilty. One boy tried to suggest the hamster had escaped and climbed up the table leg and got through the whole drilled for the spilled ink to drain. A good idea I thought so keep thinking that I thought. Then some one asked how did it get out of the cage as the door was closed. I was feeling very, very guilty now and wondered if Miss Kitchinger was thinking had I done the deed the night before. I kept quiet and to this day they do not know how that hamster got there.

During this time my brother was attending the Lea Farm Junior School, the school I was to attend the next year or so.

Congregational Sunday School

My mum use to take me to Sunday school from time to time and I didn't mind going. One day (about 1958) on the way home from normal school I would walk past the Congregational Church Building, rather a modern building, and the vicar lived in a Gypsy stile caravan in the church grounds.

Garston Congregational Church Building

Congregational Church Building

The church building was always left open and we often went in the building on the way home. I saw, on one occasion, some boys took the money out of the collection box, which too was left unlocked. I could not understand this. Why where things left unlocked for boys to steel from. One day, after school, I met the vicar when I was looking around the church building and I asked him why is the building left open and why it the collection box not locked. His reply puzzled me. He said the church should be always open for people because God was like that if people felt they need to steel the collection then they must need it badly. He did not feel the box should be locked. I was puzzled and said but why? The vicar was sure it was the right thing to do. That stayed with me to this day and people get angry some times with me for not locking up my house.

What Was Easter All About ?

At this same church I can remember the Easter services. I had no Idea what the gospel was nor did I understand the Easter story.

I remember sitting in the pew during the Easter service listening to how they crucified Jesus wondering why Jesus did not come down from the cross. I felt he could have done so and confounded all them Pharisees, but why didn't he do so. I knew the story about his death and resurrection but did not know what it all meant. I never did find out until 14 years later when I was 21 years old after I learned to read the bible for my self. It was then I learned that Jesus had to die to take away my sins. That he died in my place to set me free from sin, self and death.

It was about this time (1959) that my mum encouraged me to play the piano. My mum's favourite artist was Perry Como and "Side Saddle" was a piece of mum's favourite music, which I learned to play. I had music lesson with a Miss Mary Lee, a music teacher in Garston and eventually I graduated with a merit Grade 1 (Primary) RSA in Pianoforte. This was July 1960.

The sort of music, which was popular in those days, was. "Yellow Polka Dot Bikini, My Old mans a dustman, by Lonnie Donnigan, Living Doll by Cliff Richards. Also the Hula-Hoop was a craze at that time.

Cecil The Sissy And Air Pistol

Living not too far away from us in Coats Way, was a boy who my brother nicknamed Cecil, as this sounded like a suitable name for a sissy. He was a cripple in the sense that his feet were curved inwards and he walked awkwardly. He must have been about 10 years old. My brother poked fun at him and I too soon followed suit. We would sing about him a song called Cecil, Cecil a Cecil feet. He would try and avoid us.

One day Cecil came on his bike down to the woods that we called the dell. We were playing up the trees and had made a catapult out off one of the great branches of the trees. One person would sit in the branch and two or three other kids would pull on the rope till the branch was fully bent. The rope would be released and the person would be catapulted up in the air. They would have to hold on tightly other wise they would end up in the trees.

On this day my brother had it in for Cecil. We took his bike and put it into the catapult making sure it was catapulted up into the trees. We thought this was great fun but Cecil did not.

His mother came to our house and complained to my mum about our bullying Cecil but my mum seemed to have no mercy. She said Cecil had got to learn to look after himself and he was a sissy. I felt mum was wrong as I knew how bad we were and my mum seemed to have no mercy. I felt bad however.

Shortly after this incident my brother encouraged me to take our newly acquired air pistol to school, and Cecil was the one who my brother bullied and threaten to shoot in the playground. On reflection my brother seemed to have no mercy at all. Michael must have been in the final year and I in the first year of Lea Farm Junior School.

David at Lea Farm Junior School

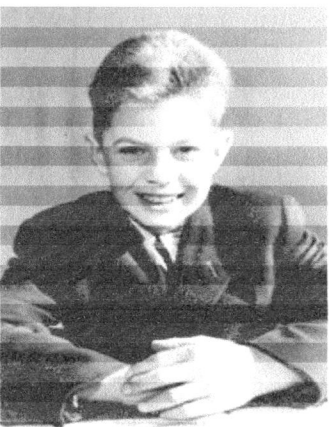

David at Lea Farm Junior School

It wasn't long however before my air pistol was found and confiscated. After assembly one of the boys had taken it out of my desk and was running around the classroom with it when the teacher walked in. I was in trouble again with the Headmaster and this would have been another time I got the cane for bringing a dangerous weapon to school.

I Get Electrocuted And Burned

During this time, one day I was not well, and stayed at home, whilst my mum went to work. It was cold and all the heating we had was a one bar electric fire. At this time I was sitting on a chair in our lounge trying to read but drifted off to sleep. My arm fell down onto the fire element and I was electrocuted. I was unconscious and when I came too my hand burned so much I was in real pain. All I could do was to remember what to do. I run my hand under the cold tap and then wrapped my hand in a tea towel. I was about 8 or 9 years old. I decided to catch the bus and go to my mum, who was working at Watford Peace Memorial Hospital. When I arrived she wondered just what I was doing at her work, and when I showed her my hand she realised I need help. All my fingers were burned severely and I needed treatment. In fact it was serious because I could have been killed by the electric shock as I was knocked unconscious and could have been stuck to the electric fire element powered by 240 volts a.c.

Wrexham Holiday

Michael and I must have been about 7 and 10 years old and Mum and dad had renovated an old Ford convertible car whose number plate was BBU.

Mum had bought the car whilst we were living in Oldham and dad was working in Watford. Dad had moved to Watford to get a job, and was living with his mum (our grandma at Ash Tree Road Garston, Watford). Mum and dad were able to by a house at 149 Coats Way Garston and it was mum who decided to buy the car to get Michael and I down from Oldham to Watford.

It was this car that I often fell out of when the breaks were hit. It caused me to move forward and push open the door lock and the door opened the opposite way round. I would end up on the road outside the car. Dad eventually was able to put a safety chain on the handle to stop this happening.

Dad had rebuilt the engine and painted it black and green, Mum made a new convertible top using her sewing skills. It was a bit like Noddy's car it was really good.

In this car we went to Brixton for a holiday and it was there mum and dad bought Michael and I a fishing rod each. I had a wooden cane one and he had a metal rod. I remember I was always jealous of what he had as I always thought his things were better than mine.

Keen to try the rods out near the sea harbour Michael rushed to the waterside just around the corner and soon came back crying. He said a man had taken his rod and thrown it into the sea. Dad rushed around but no one could be seen. We looked for the man on his bike but no one was to be seen. It is only now that I look back that I believe Michael had quickly put the rod together pretended to fish by casting an imaginary line and the rod top had gone straight into the see. He probably felt he would have been told off by our dad and be in trouble. So he invented a story about a man on a bike.

When I look back it is incidences like this that I learned about the way Michael thought and worked and in later life it made one wonders at the tales he told.

The Fair At Garston, Paper Round And Stolen Bike

Every year the fair would come to Garston and I really looked forward to ride the dodgem cars. All the kids would go to the fair and spend lots of time watching. I can remember two brothers who worked on the fair and these were like heroes, and we would wonder who was the strongest and speculate which one could lift a dodgem car above his head. We would also listen to the latest pop music, which played through large loudspeakers. This was before any one had personal radios or cassette players. There was no Top of the Pops on T.V.. So the fair was the only place to hear pop music.

I was probably about 11 or 12 years old, and this year I remember stealing £3 from my mum's purse. I felt very guilty and bad at the time and I still feel the shame as I write about it now, but this was spent on the fair. I am thankful for the truth that the blood of Jesus cleanses us from all sin. This became my only way of me dealing with my sin when I became a Christian and still is.

Don't Talk To Strangers

I loved the fair and would go as often as I could. However one day, a man dressed in a suit, offered me free rides in the dodgem cars, and whilst I thought it a bit odd I gladly took advantage of the free rides. This man than asked me if I could help him as his car had broken down, and it was just along the St. Albans Road. I realised this was more than odd so I managed to slip away. At the time I didn't realise the kind of danger that I had been in, but when I told my mum she soon had the police around, and I gave a description of the man to them. My mum and dad said no more about the matter except not to talk to strangers. It was only later in life that I realised the ways of paedophiles and the warning is to young people, or any one, don't talk to strangers.

Playing Truant From School

One rainy day whilst walking to school with Michael Abbes we decided not to go to school and play truant. We spent the miserable, wet, day walking in the woods and going with out food. I had no real need not to go to school but it was Michael who didn't want to go.

Any way the next day we were asked independently why had we not been to school, and I felt it necessary to tell the truth. I had played truant. Michael Abbes had said he was sick and had got his mother to write a note to that effect. Needless to say I was caned for playing truant and Michael Abbes got off scot free. I felt that it was unjust and felt that I had been punished for telling the truth. I was not happy.

Money Buys Many Things

My brother at that time had a paper round and use to get up early each morning and so he began to earn his own money. I remember him obtaining all sorts of new things like writing cases, pens, pencils, ink cartridges, etc. And all the little things one would like but could not afford. I soon realized that my brother was not buying them but stealing them from the shop where he worked.

On the odd occasion I would go and help him deliver the papers.

I enjoyed this as it took me to places that I had never been before.

On one occasion we had to deliver papers to a hospital or residential home, and around the back of the building we could see the kitchens and we helped our selves to the cakes, which had been freshly cooked. I learn from my brother how easy it was to get things I wanted.

I always looked up to my brother and often envied the things he did and had. I remember him going to Switzerland, with the school and coming home with all kinds of goods. Like a walking stick, flick knives, and badges etc. Flick knives were illegal and to have a flick knife was a good thing.

My brother soon got in to bows and arrows, and air rifles and pistols, catapults, swords and sheath knives, which seemed good to me. In fact we use to hide all these weapons under the floorboards in our shed, which was at the bottom of our garden.

At this time I remember my mum and dad buying me a new bike. It was a red Californian, with curved crossbars etc. I thought it was great and was ever so pleased with it. One day the bike went missing, and I knew some one had taken it, so I was very upset.

When I went out looking for it I noticed up the road an accident had taken place, as there were cars stopped and people milling around. To my horror I saw my nice new bike crumpled and just lying at the side of the road. The boy who had taken it had been knocked off the bike and was lying in the road awaiting an ambulance and every one was trying to take care of him.

I thought to my self never mind about him, as he had stolen my bike, but look at my new bike, all bent. I was very upset. No one however took any notice of me, neither were they concerned about my bike being damaged. The boy's name was Michael Abbes and we had been friends until recently and I seem to remember that he had broken his legs in the accident.

Stolen Crystal Set

My interest in radio, which we now call electronics, started the day I heard a crystal set operate. I must have been 10 or 11 years old.

My mum and dad belonged to the Camping Club of Great Britain and every weekend we would go camping to Chertsey, where we had a tent pitched.

Camping at Chertsey

Dad at Chertsey campsite Dad by our Canoe

One weekend my brother stole a crystal set from a camper's tent. It consisted of a small tuning capacitor in a blue plastic case and a crystal diode, together with a set of headphones. I was amazed as it worked and became interested in radio from that day forward.

I sent away for a set of parts to build a two transistor reflex receiver, and put the thing together as best I could. I wired the circuit as I thought the diagram showed, and crushed it all together to fit inside its plastic case. It didn't work and I was most disappointed. I didn't realize that all the wires were shorted together when I crushed it into the plastic case. Another friend of mine's dad helped me out. He was a radio technician in the Royal Air force and he rebuilt the receiver and showed me how to wire circuits up. From that time I began to learn about how things worked and taught my self-many things with the help of others.

Another friend of mine had a dad who had a radio workshop and I was very envious of all the equipment that he had in his garage. I remember the boy being confident enough to take apart out of an old radio for me, without any sense of fear. I was quite impressed. I taught my self quite a lot and began to learn about transistors.

Stealing Radio Equipment

One day on the way home from school we climbed over the fence of someone's back garden and discovered a shed full of radio parts, and equipment. There were valves, tuning condensers, transformers etc., We took what we wanted and thought no more of it.

This hobby was to last me a long time and helped me to get a job in Radio and Television Servicing and to Technical College at a later date. During this time I had no sense or knowledge of God and I had stopped going to Sunday school.

A Visit From The Police

About this time I manage to break into a work mans hut which was at the gravel pit situated on not to far from our home. Me along with other kid would play there during the evening and climb on top of the work mans working shed. There were also two large tanks of hot water and we would after dangle our feet in the water and wash our selves after getting dirty. On this occasion we managed to break in the shed and I managed to steal a wireless receiver. It was a valve receiver in a wooden box. I took it to pieces and saved the chassis and had it in my bedroom at Coats Way. Some how the police were tipped off and they came and searched our house for the stolen goods. I was thankful I had got rid of the wooden cabinet as they found no evidence of the break in.

Francis Coombe Secondary School

My first senior school was in Garston, as I had failed the 11 plus. It was at this school I first heard a boy play a tune called , "Apache" by the Shadows, on an acoustic guitar and I was very impressed. Michael had already started at this school and did well at cricket, boxing and basketball. I was not good at any of these things but rather was interested in my radio hobby, which led me to trips to London on the train, from Watford Junction, to buy components in Tottenham Court Road.

Michael and Boxing

I soon learned the my brother had a reputation at school as a boxer and I recall attending the school competition for sports and Michael won the boxing at that event. He would have been in the fourth year and about to leave school. On that occasion my uncle John and Dad were there and Uncle John after Michael's win went and congratulated the looser, in order to keep him encouraged. Parents were like that in those days.

Michael at Butlin's

Michael In The Horizontal Striped Jumper

The Senior Clarke Brothers

Uncle John and my Dad Tom Clarke

My visit to Soho

It was towards the end of my first year, at Francis Coombe Secondary Modern school, that I ventured out to London on the train, with a friend of mine, Paul Dorrington. This was to visit the second hand electrical shops, to buy radio parts. I loved visiting Tottenham Court Road for this purpose and it was on one of these visits that we stumbled across Soho and noticed the strip clubs.

These aroused our curiosity. Paul and I plucked up courage and paid to go in and sit at a table. We could see a nude lady sitting on a chair and were given a sketch pad and pencil and encouraged to draw her picture. I felt I was growing up. Afterwards we paid one or two more visits and became wiser.

When we moved to Wilstone, a village near Tring in Hertfordshire, my radio and television hobby helped me pass the time and keet me out of too much trouble

Our Move To Wilstone

In 1961 we finally moved to Wilstone a village near Tring and Michael and I went to Tring Secondary modern school called Mortimer Hill. I can remember my brother wearing winkle picker shoes and some of the girls from the next village couldn't help but say oh look at those shoes. They were just different and I suppose they felt threatened.

It was during this time that I taught myself more about Radio and amplifiers and became absorbed in this hobby. I met a man in the village called Cluck Turney, who was the man to know about televisions and radios and he gave me a lot of help. He taught me about valve amplifiers and allowed me to build a power amplifier, from all the spare parts that he had. It was a push pull amplifier using two PX4 valves and a triode driver. I had to rewind the driver and output transformers in order to get it working. I learned a lot from Cluck Turney.

On one occasion I was able to connect a microphone up to my amplifier and I directed the speaker out of my bedroom window and spoke to people out side our shop. On this occasion I saw a woman in her rear garden called Ethel. I called out with the amplifier as loud as possible saying Ethel, Ethel I am watching you. I heard many years later that she thought it sounded a bit like God speaking from the sky.

Keeping Myself Busy

To occupy myself I made things of interest. I made a kart with a large wind sale. A pair of stilts and all the kids in the village wanted a pair. On one occasion I made an electric shock machine from an ignition coil a battery and a mechanical vibrating mechanism used in an electric bell. I tested it out on the kids in the village by getting them to hold hands, in a circle and one kid at each end of the circle held the electrode. When I switched the machine on they all got a sharp electric shock. It was a success.

Stolen Shot Gun

Stolen Shot Gun From the Farm

I later had a visit from the local policeman as I had stolen a 12-bore shotgun from an old barn and brought it home. When I showed it to my next-door neighbour he recognised the gun and realised who it belonged too and so he informed the local policeman to get it returned to its owner.

Whilst at Tring School a friend of mine Duncan Miller found a baby fox cub in a wood, and I wanted to keep it so I took it home. Unfortunately my Grandma, who had come to stay, freaked out when she saw it as she was frightened and to my dismay my brother killed it and to this day I felt he was callous.

Michael at Tring School

Michael With His Friend Notice the Winkle Picker Shoes

I Ride A 350 cc Triumph

My brother mixed with all the lads who had bad reputations and no one would dare up set them and he was in the final year at Tring Secondary Modern school. He was friends with all the lads who were in trouble.

One friend was Bod Shearer, who lived on a farm in Tring and I recall Michael having an old 350 cc. Triumph motor bike, with girder front forks. I took courage and rod this bike in the field and was quite pease with myself for having the courage to riding such a big bike. I had, until that time, only ridden a moped.

The Motorbike

Michael's 350 CC Triumph Motorbike

It was during this time at Wilstone my brother got sent to his first spell in Detention Centre. He had made a knuckle-duster at school, in the metal work classes, and tried it out by hitting some boy in the village. What happened was some lads had found our moped in the field and had a go at riding it without our permission. Not that they would know whom to ask, but my brother felt he would sort them out for riding it. I think it was an excuse to use the knuckle-duster he had made.

When the police were called in he made out the knuckle duster was made as a part for the moped and my mum was certain this was true and she defended my brother to the hilt. I knew it wasn't true and my brother did a spell in Oxford Detention centre for 3 months, for grievous bodily harm. I did not go along with my brothers' violence and could not understand it. His reputation spread and at school the teachers began to identify me with my brother and I think they began to be wary of me too.

The Moped

Our Moped in Wilstone Field

Village life proved too much for my mum and she became depressed, due to they way things were, and the trouble Michael had gotten into so it was decided to sell up and move to a new house in Aylesbury.

9 The Big Freeze 1962

Once we had sold the village shop mum and I moved to Oldham whilst Michael and my dad moved into lodgings in Aston Clinton. This was while the house they had bought off plan was being built. Mum and moved to live with my aunt Edith at 26 Fleet Street, in the town where I was born and had I to go to school. This was Clark's Field Senior School and I became a bit of a celebrity simply because I was from "London". This status increased when I told the "lads" about my trips to Soho. It was here that I first heard of the Beatles as they were playing in Oldham at that time. The song I remember that was popular, "Love me do", which came out in October 1962.

During my time in Oldham we were there for about three months, I built a balsa wood, controlled line, aeroplane, a radio transmitter for a remote control aircraft and learned to ice skate. We had a very cold winter, the coldest on record and the snow fell and the streets froze over. My mum bought me a pair of second hand ice skates and I learned to skate on the frozen streets in Oldham.

Short Stay Back To Watford

After staying for while in Oldham we moved back to Watford and lived with my Dad's mum. On this occasion I had to go back to Francis Coombe Secondary School and I renewed acquaintances with my school old friends. It was during this time I made my own transistor radio set.

I also missed riding the moped and so I got up very early one morning and walked into Watford where I knew a motorbike was parked and stole it. I drove several miles to a secret place and parked it and went home. I later used it for joy riding with my friends. I walked miles that morning and my mum never knew about it.

Michael also would visit us at Watford and see his old friends who played in a pop group and on one occasion he gave me a pair of bell-bottom trousers and a shirt, with a long pointed collar. Michael and his friend wanted to take me to the dance that was held at Leavesdon, on a Friday or Saturday night. I really enjoyed myself there and wanted to go again. I met some of my friends from school there and one boy noticed my clothes and said that I was a Mod.

Unfortunately for me after this I began to get bullied at school by a group of boys who were what you might call "Jack the Lads". I learned afterward the reason and it was to do with Michael. One of the boys was from Australia and was the ringleader of this gang and he had a girl friend at the school called Pat Petty. She was every boy's dream of a girl. Well Michael had met her at the Leavesdon dance and chatted her up. This Australian boy was jealous and a soon as they realised that I was Michael's brother they had it in for me.

My First Matchbox Radio

This is the radio that I made and obtained a circuit diagram for a two transistor reflex receiver and with the components I obtained from Tottenham Court Road, in London, I built this on a small paxolin board. This was before printed circuit boards were readily available. I was very pleased with this as it had good sensitivity and selectivity and was about the size of a matchbox.

My Two Transistor Wireless Receiver

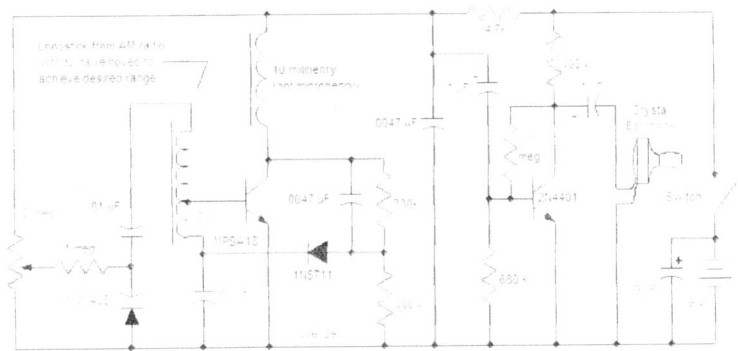

Here Is The Circuit Diagram

A Holiday in Newquay

At this time Mum and Dad took me and my sister Margaret, who was about 3 years old, to Newquay for a holiday. I didn't know what kind of place it was but when we got there it was great. The sand the sea and the surfing and views were a treat to see. It was here that I conducted my first blag (a scheme or scam) as I wanted to explore the Headland Hotel, which was an impressive hotel.

The Hotel

Anyway on this occasion I took Margaret by the hand and we walked down the drive right into the hotel. As we approached a steward of some kind came up to me and asked if he could help. I confidentially replied no thank we are staying here. He stood upright, in embarrassment and said, oh yes I remember the little girl. So we blagged it and I wondered around the hotel with my 3 year old sister, admiring the hotel.

This Is The Hotel Where The Film The Witches Were Filmed

The Headlands Hotel Newquay

My brother and I returned to Newquay for a holiday in 1967 just before we were both sent to prison.

Aylesbury: Our New Home

Our new house was situated on the Bedgrove Estate, in Aylesbury and was ready for us to move in April of 1963. However before we left Wilstone I had enjoyed riding a moped in an old orchard, in the village. It belonged to a friend of Michael and I was allowed to ride this moped. It was a 50 cc NSU Quickly and was kept in his orchard.

Once we had moved into out new house in Aylesbury I was able to return to Wilstone and take the engine from the moped frame and put the engine in a home made go kart. I made this go- kart from builder's wood that I took from the building site. I use the moped engine, a set of wheels from a child's three wheeler tricycle, and various parts from a cement mixer. I then began to ride this machine around the new roads on the housing estate. However I was eventually stopped by the local police and warned that it was illegal to ride this Go Kart on the roads and soon after that the local newspaper came and gave me a write up in local paper.

Bucks Herald News Article

An Aylesbury boy was able to return to school after the Easter holidays and proudly tell his friends, " I've made a Go Cart in the holidays." He is 14 years old,

On Sunday of last week a friend gave David (pictured above) and old moped. As he was unable to ride it as he is too young he dismantled it. He then made a Kart frame from some pieces of wood, four old wheels and a set of handlebars and the moped engine.

Within three days it was in working condition and David estimates it will do 20 miles and hour.

Incidentally David, who has lived in the town for only a month has very little real interest in engines. His main hobby is in radio construction work and one of his proudest possessions is a transistor radio, which he built that is slightly larger than a matchbox.

David's Do It Your Self-Kart

David's Do it Your Self Kart (May 1963)

I Steel Push Bikes

It was during this space of time, before starting my new school; I met another lad called Ian Motram. We encouraged each other to steel . In fact the first day that I went to school I stole a bike to come home from school.

I eventually got a Francis Barnet 150 CC motorbike, which my brother had stolen from Aylesbury College, with some other lads. I kept this in a field on the Bedgrove Estate near our home.

It was great fun to have a motorbike and I would ride across the fields to school and return home during my lunch hour.

The NSU Quickly Moped

My Moped

However one day some one stole my motorbike and Ian Motram informed me that he thought he knew the person that had taken it. I went to this person's house early one morning, during my paper round, and found a motorbike in his garage. This wasn't my bike but I took it anyway. This ended up in me being charge with garage breaking and being put on probation for two years.

Stolen Francis Barnett 150 CC Motor Bike

My Francis Barnett Motor Bike

10 I Meet Mrs Grace Knight

My teenage years

My first recollection of any religious person having any effect on my life was when I was about to leave school, at the age of 15 years old.

My mother had spoken to a Mr K H Knight who was the proprietor of Central Bucks T.V. and had arranged for me to have a part time job working after school and on a Saturday. This was until I left school and took up full time work as an apprentice to Mr Knight.

I am told years later that my letter of job application was so badly written and the spelling so awful it was laughable. However I was taken on despite my inability to write, spell or use correct grammar, or read properly. This was during my last year at school.

I first met Mrs Grace Knight, one Saturday morning, whilst working for her husband Ken. She was in hot pursuit of Ken and shouting at him for doing some thing she disapproved of.

I was in the workshop, with Norman Garret the other apprentice, and I thought- wow what an awful dragon of a woman and pitied Mr Knight from that moment on.

Through Mr Knight I was introduced to the Radio and Television servicing trade and often went with him into customer's houses to repair T.V.'s and install television aerials.

I spent many hours with Ken going to peoples homes and soon learned that he was not faithful to his wife. Not that it bothered me, as I knew what Grace was like from our first meeting. The idea of sexual promiscuity was very attractive to me. When we went out enjoying our selves Mrs Knight would be left at home or in the workshop minding their two children Allison and Mark. They also had a big dog called Rufus.

By this time I had left school and was interested in our band, as we wanted to make music. Ian Myers was the bass guitarist and he built his own guitar amplifier from a circuit design and published in Practical Wireless. He built the amplifier and I helped him with the speaker cabinet and it was used in all our future gigs.

I soon began to realize the things I enjoyed were not the things Mrs Knight approved of, or found interesting. I thought she was a right "kill joy" and was boring. She was a Christian what ever that meant and I soon realize her values were not the same as mine. What I considered good and enjoyable she would call it sin and sinful. She would also complain to her husband that I was always with him and he gave her no time. It seemed she was often driven to despair by him never being in on time and being very unreliable. He would often leave her for hours whilst we were at work out on jobs.

Conversation Over The Intercom

On one occasion Norman Garret's mum complained to Mrs Knight the Norman her son, was not getting the training he needed because Ken was always taking me out with him. I heard this conversation over the shops intercom. Mrs Knight said yes I was a nuisance and she did not like me one bit and it was not good that I should be out with her husband all the time. Upon hearing this I felt angry and went down the stairs to where they were and confronted them both saying that I had heard what they had said about me. They were embarrassed and I am sure this did not help our relationship. I really thought Mrs Knight was an ogre.

I began to attend Luton College of Technology, to learn about Radio and Television Servicing, and travelled by bus, one day a week, from Aylesbury to Luton; it was about an hour and a half run. I think it must have been due to Mrs Knight and her religion that I began to notice the texts of scripture put up out side churches as I past by on the bus, they were called "Way Side Pulpits". I began to memorize the verses such as:

" Righteousness exalteth a nation but sin is a reproach to any people"

And also another:

" Jesus said if you find life difficult learn of me and the burden I shall give you will not be too difficult to carry".

At that time I had no idea of the meaning of these texts of scripture but found it amusing to quote them to Mrs Knight at any inappropriate moment, in public, thinking it would embarrass her.

On one occasion I remember being dressed in an old blanket made into an undercoat from my brothers Mod anorak. I was standing on the corner of the street near to the workshop one Saturday morning with Mr and Mrs Knight. I quoted at the top of my voice these two scriptures in order to embarrass Mrs Knight. I am not sure how they felt about it but little did I know that one day I would learn the truth of these texts and become a preacher of the Gospel myself and this quotation contained the essence of gospel ministry.

Mrs Grace Knight became a great help to me and lived until 2001. Here is a link to a video of her funeral.

Obituary Grace Maude Knight

(Click to view)

1 Driving to the Funeral

2 Grace Knight David Obituary

3 Grace Knight Ken's Obituary

4 Graces Funeral John Knight Obituary

5 Grace Mark Knight's Obituary

6 Graces Funeral The Burial

A Confident 15 year old

I enjoyed working for Mr Knight because he seemed to appreciate my help and abilities and would trust me to drive the van at 15 years old. On one occasion he was short of a driver and had to deliver a television. So he dressed me up in a sheepskin coat and gave me dark glasses to wear with instructions to deliver a T.V. to a house in Quarendon. I was very pleased to do this even more when it turned out that I was delivering the T.V. set to one of my school friends called Gillespie.

On another occasion I was given the job of replacing a complete I.F. board on a new Ferguson 850 T.V. Receiver in a customers home. A qualified engineer in a workshop setting normally would have done this but this unconventional approach was normal to me. Mr Knight had complete confidence in me at the age of 15 years old. I am sure the customer was not at all happy at this 15 year old repairing their lovely brand new television receiver.

During this time I was still making music in the group and when I was 16 Mr Knight's business failed and went into liquidation so I found myself another job. I got an apprenticeship with Sale and Mellor at a Radio a T.V. shop in Aylesbury. I worked there until I got in trouble with the police when I was sacked at the age of 17 years.

It was shortly after this time that I got into trouble with the police for breaking into a garage and stealing a motorbike. I had a Francis Barnett 150 CC, which had been stolen from the field where I kept it and a friend of mine told me that it was in this garage, along the Tring Road. At first I was just interested in getting my bike back but when I opened the garage door I was disappointed not to find it - just a 125 BSA Bantam.

Stolen BSA Bantem

BSA Bantem 125 CC Motor Bike

I thought well its better than nothing so I decided to take it any way and wheeled it out of the garage and back to our field, to use it later. The police later caught me and for this first crime I was charged with garage breaking and put on probation for two years.

11 Our Rock Group

It was after this that decided I wanted to play the electric guitar and I remember a lad called Alan Lawrence, from Tring Secondary Modern School, having an electric guitar and bringing it to school. He plugged it into the schools record player and it sounded great. I wanted to learn to play like him. The first guitar I owned was an electric Hofner Futurama Two and a friend called Steve showed me how to play Twist and Shout and it was this that got me really interested to play properly. I put together my own guitar amplifier, using the P. A. Amplifier that I had stolen from the Catholic Church.

(I had inherited a prejudice against the Catholic Church, from my mum, and so when I took the amplifier I ignored my conscience by saying to myself they were wrong any way).

I then began to get more interested in making music and during my last year at school we formed a band and we played at the end of term school dance. Our Gym teacher, Mr Pottinger, organized this event.

Wild Willy Barrett

In the group line up was Willy Barrett on guitar and vocals. Barge Collier's younger brother, on vocals, Ian Myers, Robby Woods on guitar and Maghue on drums and me guitar.

The Fowler Mean our Rock group

After this we formed a bang called The Fowler Mean and Ian Myers was the base guitarist and later Robby Woods became our lead guitarist. Willie Barrett was the only one of us to make musical fame. He became known as Wild Willy Barrett and played music with John Ottway.

My First Guitar Amplifier

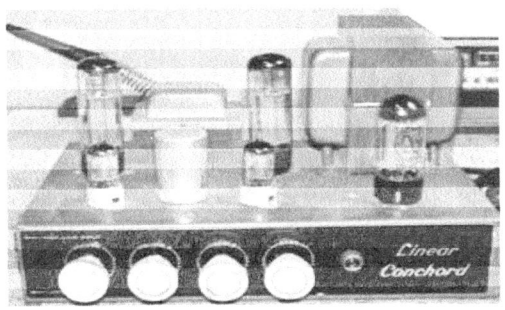

Liner Concorde 30 Amplifier

Linear Concord 30 Watt Underneath Chassis

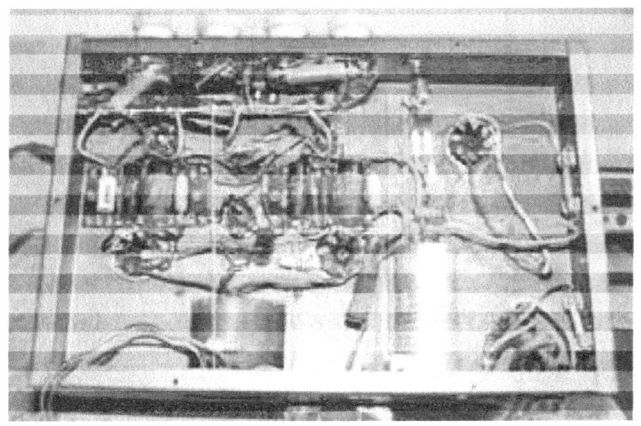

Hand Wired Main Chassis

A Secret

Willy Barrett's dad was a brilliant man, a musician and a craftsman, he made an excellent bass guitar for either Willy or his friend. He wanted an amplifier for Willie's electric guitar and the bass player friend said he had a 30 Watt Linear Concord amplifier for sale, for a small amount of money and I jumped in quickly before they made their mind up and bought it from this man. This is the one in my picture.

How ever I then agreed to sell my 15 Watt linear Concord amplifier that I had stolen from the Catholic Church, in North Watford to his dad for a little bit less money and they bought it of me. I was very pleased but felt a bit guilty because they got a rough deal and really they should have had the 30 Watt amplifier which was much better than mine. Little did they know I had stolen the amplifier.

Wild Willy Barrett

Wild Willy Barrett

Here Go to Wikipedia for Willy Barrett's Profile

Wild Willy Barrett and John Otway

Willy Barrett and John Otway (Click view)

My Vox A.C. 30 Amplifier

My Guitar Amplifier

Playing At Courts Dance School

I had a new amplifier that was a Vox A.C. 30 and replaced the amplifier that I had stolen from the Catholic Church. One of our regular spots, on a Saturday night, was Courts Dance School, just off Kingsbury Square. Here is our music play set:

The Fowler Mean (Play Set) Click to view

After leaving school we reformed the group and began to play music at various dance halls and I named the group "The Fowler Mean".

We would play all cover music by groups such as, The Rolling Stones, The Who, The Small Faces, The Kinks, Ottis Reading and John Lee Hooker. We played, "My Generation", but I knew it was not quite right and I never did find out how to play the right cords to this day. The opening chords we played were four down strokes on G followed by four downward strokes on F but that is not right.

The Fowler Mean

Dave Clarke from the 60's, with Robby Woods (top) Ian Myers

I always thought if ever I met Pete I would ask him to show me how to play those opening chords. I really enjoyed playing with the band but was eventually sacked and it was then that Malcolm Kirkham and I began to knock around with each other.

Our Favourite Band The Who

John Entwhistle, Pete Townsend, Keith Moon and Roger Daultery

My favourite band was The Who. This group introduced something to music that was new. It was volume. My Generation was the real hit that made the Who. I can remember hearing them, at the Grosvenor Dance Hall, in Aylesbury. Pete Townsend was the lead guitar, John Entwhistle on bass, Keith Moon on drums and Roger Daultary lead singer. There was not a band to touch them they were brilliant. We saw them on a number of occasions including places like Borehamwood and the Bedford Corn Exchange.

The Who (Click here to go to Wikipedia)

I remember the amplifier line up (being interest in amplifiers) Pete Townsend had:

Pete Townsend Amplifier line up

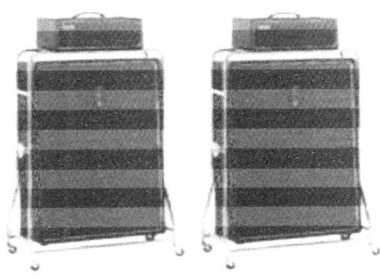

Two A.C. 100 Amplifiers in Parallel

John Entwhistle amplifier line up

John Entwhistle 4 X A.C. 60 watt Vox Bass

Amplifiers and their PA system was Vox columns and Shure microphones.

The volume added another dimension to the experience. I call it Rock and Real Music, It added depth to the sound and none of us had experienced anything like it before These are just some of the songs:

The Who Play List (click to view)

These were all classic Who numbers and none forgettable pieces of music

Malcolm Kirkham use to be one of our singers which made 5 in the band and we use to go out together on our scooters. I had inherited my brother's Lambretta T.V. 175 CC and Malcolm had a 150 CC new Lambretta and we began to mix with the Mods in Aylesbury and district.

He had been sacked from the group because he messed about. Malcolm would always arrive late and never be in time to set up the equipment. He was always combing his hair or having to press his trousers, and he general fooled around. He was nicknames Cocoa the Clown.

After mixing with the other lads in Aylesbury I soon found out my brother was well known and when it was made known I was Mick Clarke's brother it was like having a license to or say any thing, I was accepted. I was one of the boys. I recalled the times my brother had told me of the parties they use to have and I began to want to get involved in all the fun. Pep pills, scooters, Mod fashions, dances, girls and permissive sex. All of which I found positive and attractive as we were looking for a good time in the world.

The image I had of my brother was that he was quite a character and had a way with girls. I remember that was how I wanted to be and follow him in fame. I remember one impressive occasion I must have been just 16 and met one of Michael's friends who was a Mod. One Saturday night out side the Grosvenor he came dressed in brightly coloured trousers and a black plastic mac wearing girls make up around the eyes. He was Glenny Williams. This was the in thing to do and I thought this is good and liked it.

The normal mode of transport was either a Lambretta or Vespa scooter with crash bars, back rests, spare wheel carriers and mirrors. The scooters would be custom sprayed and generally a world war green Parker or black plastic cape was the uniform. All of this became the world I wanted to be in.

Oxford Bags

I remember my brother coming to see us at Rockley Sands, in Bournemouth when I was away with my parents on holiday. I must have been 15 years old. He came dressed in a brown suit with 22 inch, Oxford Bag trousers, with small turn-ups. His top was a white crew necked and red striped tea shirt. Also brown brogue leather shoes. This was some fashion that I had not seen before. It was the Mod fashion.

He told me he had to return to Aylesbury to do some repairs and tidy up mum and dads house as they had a party and the place had been wrecked. Apparently all the Aylesbury Mods and from the district had been to his party held at Mum and Dads house. They had rolled up the carpets and put them in the garage but the bathroom sink had been pulled off the wall as some girl had got drunk and sat in it. He told me of the promiscuity and it all seemed good fun. This was the year 1963 or 4 when the Beatles and Rolling Stones came to fame. Also Gerry and the Pacemakers had a hit record at the time called, "I Like it".

My First Girl Friend

I met Susan, at a Friday night dance being organized at the Aylesbury College; she was 15 years old and looked great. She had blond hair in a Bob style. I was 16, wearing my navy blue Mod suit. I had arrived on my Lambretta.

I asked her to dance and later asked if I could take her home. I was feeling great when she agreed and so I covered up my learner plate, which was just under the rear, number plate and took her home. This was the beginning of my first love. The relationship only lasted a few months. When she told me she wanted to finish the relationship I was heart broken and she sought to encourage me by saying I would find some one else. I never did and had no interest in finding any one else. My only interest in girls after that was for sex alone- not friendship or anything else.

Love is Strange

 Love Is Strange, Everly Brothers.

(click to view)

I first heard this song, by The Who, at Borehamwood

The Mod Image

Lambretta Mod Suit   Blond Girl friend Sue

During this time Malcolm and I mixed with the Mods in Aylesbury we were both 16 years old and we began to meet with these older lads and were curious to try pep pills (purple hearts, black bombers and Dexedrine) and smoke hashish, or grass, so we began to make some inquiries where to get some. In the mean time we would experiment smoking crushed codeine tablets and dried banana skins. This was purely to satisfy a curiosity and to experience new things. The was a pub in Aylesbury called the, "Flee Pit" situated in Kingsbury Square and it was there we understood we could buy hash. However at 16 years old I went in this pub and became very embarrassed as on the wall behind the bar were displayed ladies knickers in various styles and colours. I felt embarrassed because the sight aroused me as at that time there was very little pornography and the sight of a woman in a short skirt and legs was very provocative for a 16 year old, On reflection I had a very high libido. Which led to a very promiscuous life style.

Carknapping

Shortly after this I remember my brother coming home about 9.30 p.m. in a hurry. He had not long been released from Detention Centre. Our parents were away and I had a girl friend there. In came my brother and told me of his narrow escape from the police. About six of his friends had been out in a stolen car, when the police had stopped them along the Tring Road. They had all jumped out and made a run for it. It was soon after this that my brother got sent to Borstal Training for some crime or other. Never the less it all seemed a good life style and I wanted more of it.

Sniffing Chloroform

I had discovered I could buy chloroform from a chemist and this was much better than sniffing carbon Tetrachloride or the glue substances people began to experiment with. Shortly after this Malcolm Kirkham, after trying something like, this took it in his head that he could fly on his scooter. He broke his arm and smashed his scooter in the process but fortunately not his head as he was wearing a dear stalker crash helmet he had stolen a few days before.

My Lambretta Scooter

Lambretta T.V. 175 CC

The names of some of the lads we knew and come to mind were: Stuart Knight, Keith Guntrip, Ian Wilton, Dill Dorwrick, and Terry Tatem (Now dead), Phil Davis, Brian Collier, Mickey Coil, Roy Miles, John James, Dave King, Jimmy Findlay, Phil Davis, and the like all of which had one thing in common. They wanted fun and were the lads of Aylesbury. (Time of writing this is the year 2000).

Banbury Gaff

At that time after being sacked from the group we began going to a nightclub called the Banbury Gaff. Here we would stay up all night taking pep pills (we use to say getting blocked) dancing and talking and in the morning end up in a cafe eating toast before driving back to Aylesbury.

Soon after this Malcolm began to mix with the lads from Oxford and he was later sentence to some time in prison, for some crime or other. During this time my brother was in Borstal and at the Gaff, I met Alan Dodd. He was my brother's partner in crime and had escaped from Borstal. He was living on a barge in Oxford. He told me at the time, he had a gun, and all this type of living impressed me, as it seemed rather exciting. Later Michael told me that Alan Dodd had grassed him up and that was why he had got caught and sent to Borstal himself.

We would spend time at the Gaff, talking with other lads about the crimes we had done, and planned various schemes and bragged and boasted about things we had done.

From this experience of mine I can say that there is no prevention or cure from this kind of criminal mind set. Once on that route you are on the road to serious crime, as all that I knew at that time will confirm. I can also say that a girl friend could really help some one like that avoid getting into too much crime.

The Great Train Robbery

It wasn't long after the Great Train Robbery that we were finding our feet as criminals.

Bridgo Bridge

The Scene of the Robbery 1963

The great train robbery had taken place on August 8, 1963 at the

Bridgo Bridge in Linslaid, just up the road from us in Aylesbury. The thieves laid an ambush for the mail train running from Glasgow to Euston and stole more than £2 million. For 125 years, the train had run uninterrupted until that night, when it was stopped by a red light in Buckinghamshire. Bruce Reynolds who crafted the robbery, was caught in 1969 and sentenced to 10 years in jail.

We were very impressed at this crime.

The Kray Twins

In the 1960's, the Ronnie and Regie Kray were seen as prosperous and charming celebrity nightclub owners and were part of the Swinging London scene. A large part of their fame was due to their non-criminal activities as popular figures on the celebrity circuit, being photographed by David Bailey on more than one occasion; and socializing with lords, MP's, socialites and show business characters such as the actors George Raft, Judy Garland, Diana Dors, Barbara Windsor and singer Frank Sinatra.

"They were the best years of our lives. They called them the swinging sixties. The Beatles and the Rolling Stones were rulers of pop music, Carnaby Street ruled the fashion world... and me and my brother ruled London. We were fucking untouchable..." – Ronnie Kray, in his autobiographical book, My Story.

The Twins

Ronnie and Regie Kray

Kray's Imprisonment

On 8 May 1968, the Kray's and 15 other members of their firm were arrested. Many witnesses came forward now that the Kray's' reign of intimidation was over, and it was relatively easy to gain a conviction.

The Kray's and 14 others were convicted, with one member of the firm being acquitted. One of the firm members that provided a lot of the information to the police was arrested yet only for a short period.

Out of the 17 official firm members, 16 were arrested and convicted.

The twins' defence, under their counsel John Platts-mills, QC, consisted of flat denials of all charges and the discrediting of witnesses by pointing out their criminal past. The judge, Mr Justice Melford Stevenson said: "In my view, society has earned a rest from your activities." Both were sentenced to life imprisonment, with a non-parole period of 30 years for the murders of Cornell and Mcvitie, the longest sentences ever passed at the Old Bailey, (Central Criminal Court, London) for murder. Their brother Charlie was jailed for 10 years for his part in the murders.

Reputation Was Important

The Kray twins were older than us, but their reputation was significant to us. They were in their early 40's and I was just 17 and Michael 20 years old when we got sent to prison. I admired their life style and the way they conducted themselves. Both Michael and I were to follow suit.

Mods, Rockers, Scooters, Bikes a Bubble Car

Shortly after my brother came out of Borstal a form of transport was required for two. The solution to this came through my brother who persuaded me to swap my scooter for a two-seater, Issetta 300 cc bubble car. I had inherited the scooter from my Michael when he was sent to Borstal but by now it had been renovated. I had rebuilt it in the spare bedroom at home and re sprayed it British racing Green. It was a Lambretta T.V. 175 cc. The fuel tank and tool compartment was stove enamelled gold. It had a dual seat with a passenger back rest with very little extras. There had been crazes whereby crash bars, wing mirrors, wheel racks and anything made of chrome were generally attached to such machines, but not mine. I was proud of this Lambretta. It had to go to make way for the sky blue Bubble Car.

Pete Townsend Gives Us A Lift

Before this time we had to thumb lifts, to get to where we wanted too if the scooter was out of action. On one occasion we were keen to get to Bedford, as The Who were playing at the Corn Exchange. We were dressed in our Mod mohair suits. Michael's a navy blue suit and mine a tan colour, and carried a small suitcase with our night things in. We got as far as Ampthill and were stuck at the corner of the Ampthill to Bedford road and were about 20 miles from Bedford. We were stuck and Michael went into a pub to get a drink whilst I stayed on the corner trying to thumb a lift as my brother needed a lift as well. To my relief and just after Michael had gone to the pub, a two seater red coupe Jaguar pulled up to offer me a lift. I rushed up to the window of the car, carrying our small suit case, feeling very relieved that I had a lift, but at the same time anxious as my brother was still in the pub. I said to the driver cheekily would he mind waiting a minute, The driver was fine and said OK. However to my surprise and amazement I realized whom the driver was it was Pete Townsend, the lead guitarist of The Who. Of course that made our day. By this Time Michael had arrived and we both squeezed into the front seat of Pete's Jaguar. We told him who we were and that we were off to Bedford to their gig at the Corn Exchange.

Pete Townsend's Jaguar

Pete Townsend MK1 Jaguar

Road Runner by The Who (Click to view)

You can imagine listening to this song driving Pete's Car.

As we drove into Bedford we stopped and Pete asked me to ask some girls the directions to where The Who were playing. Sure enough they knew and pointed us in the direction of the Corn Exchange. It was a great evening.

The Bubble Car

The bubble car at one time belonged to David Ness , of Chiltern avenue in Aylesbury, who had been given it by his brother. There was only one thing wrong with it. We had to bump start it as the starter motor did not work. (Push it and the put it in gear and jump in once the engine had started).

In this vehicle we had many adventures because we were liberated from the two wheeled scooter and could cram four people in this vehicle, if we wanted. Neither of us had passed our driving test to drive a normal car but I had past my test to drive a motorbike and my license allowed me to drive the three wheeler bubble car.

Issetta Bubble Car

300 cc Engine And Reverse Gear

Dr Clarke's Case

Whilst Michael was in Borstal, he had made for me a wooden case, like a brief case, that he had written on the side, Dr Clarke. This was for a bit of fun. However I carried, in that case, a bottle of Chloroform, whiskey and a fake gun (it was a starter pistol that fired blanks and looked real). We used the case to frighten people , as they soon learned what was inside the case.

Dr Clarke Case

On one occasion we went into the Crombie shop , just off Kingsbury Square intending to frighten the manager of the shop.

What had happened was that I had a blue mohair navy suit made to measure by him . How ever the jacket did not fit right and even after many alterations it did not fit properly. This was whilst Michael was in Borstal. So on Michael's release, and him hearing about the suit, we decided to go an get our own back and frighten the manager to pieces. He was about 21 years old and we were younger. So we went into the shop and put Dr Clarke's case on the counter and proceeded to get the chloroform out of the case intending to put the manager to sleep. We had no other intentions but simply to frighten him. When he realised what was about to take place, he was terrified and I had to stop Michael from knocking him out with the Chloroform.

Adventures In The Bubble Car

We were able to carry blankets spare clothing etc. All in the dry. We carried all that we needed for a night out in that case. It was ideal for catching girls. The front opened up and it could be driven with the front door open. **Our Bubble Car**

Front Loader 300 BMW Issetta Bubble Car

All we did was drive up to the bird we wanted to catch and stop in front of her. Open up the door and drive forward. She had no option but to fall in and we would drive off with her in the car. It was questioned was any girl safe with us around.

Having a Crack

This is what we called having a laugh and our infamy began to grow in Aylesbury among those whom we considered the lads.

On one occasion Michael and I had discovered a store of beer and bottled drink, hidden near a pub in Aylesbury's Crown pub. We helped our selves to this drink and took it upon our selves to lay claim to it. How ever one lad, Brian Sale saw our drink and went and told all the other lads that were outside the pub. At this I saw red and had to deal with the situation because all the other lads went and helped themselves to OUR store of beer. I felt quite right to hit this lad Brian Sale, so that was what I did, in front of all his mates, and I knocked him to the ground.

Off to Margate Bank Holiday

On one occasion we set off to Margate, on one Bank holiday. This was a custom amongst our generation of Mods. We all seemed to migrate to Yarmouth, Margate or Brighton. This was Whitsun bank holiday.

Webley air gun and the Bubble Car

1966 and Mod and Rocker riots were common. On this trip to the coast my brother was true to form he had borrowed a 22 Webley air pistol, from Pat Jones and was determined to have a good time and he took pot shots a people which was his way of having fun. This was not what I would have normally done because I could recall an incident that took place, on my way home from Lea Farm junior School , in Garston, when I was 12 years old. Some teenagers were having real gun fights in the woods, with air pistols and I felt how dangerous and wrong they were.

I also remembered the incident with Michael and the air gun, that I write bole in chapter 6 under the heading, "Cecil and the air pistol". How wrong that was.

However her was my brother older than I acting fearlessly. I just went along with it suppressing my natural cautiousness.

As we past through the various towns in London the air pistol was used to cause alarm. (As I write I shrivel up at the thought of what was done) We found it amusing to shoot at ladies bottoms as their reactions of shock was funny. As we passed through Lewisham several people must have reported the mystery air gun shooter and at least one lady was wounded.

Caught by the Police

Traffic police on route to Margate stopped us. These men briefly searched our car but found nothing suspicious and let us go. My brother had hidden the pistol just in time and we did not allow this close shave stop our adventure. Persons (girls) bathing at night were targets for our folly and we found it amusing to see and here a scream from a female. It was not intended to wound or harm but that really was inevitable.

During this weekend we moved on to Ramsgate and again moved with a spirit of naughtiness decided to steel a tray of peaches from a fruit and vegetable shop. The bubble car was to be used as the get away car. The shop was half way down a hill with houses on either side of the road, it was decided I should take the peaches and my brother to drive the get away car. I lifted the tray of peaches and jumped in the car as it rolled down the hill making a chug, chug, noise-attracting attention. This was our idea of a blag. Naturally we were spotted and reports were made to the police but we did not know this.

All Coppers Are Bastards

Our foolishness was brought to an end when the same traffic police that had stopped us in London, on the way home, picked us up. I could tell from their faces, like a smirk smile, that they had it in for us. This left us with a feeling that was commonly reported in our day that All Coppers were bastards. A quick search of our vehicle revealed a stolen handbag. If only we had got rid of it, I thought. Then the air gun pellets and finally the air gun itself. That was it we were arrested, the policemen having a snarl on his face and almost laughing at us. We were charge with malicious wounding and two cases of stealing. A woman in Lewisham had been travelling in a side car and been hit in the neck by the air pistol by my brother.

I was granted bail but my brother detained in custody. We had decided that I would say that I had done the shooting and my brother was a sleep. This was to get my brother off a prison sentence as he had already done two spells in detention centres, and two years in Borstal. I had only had a probation order and had an apprenticeship. I thought I would only get a fine but I was wrong.

Our Mum managed to obtain bail for my brother and we appeared in Kent Quarter sessions several months later.

On recollection I can remember a prison officer, at the Rochester Borstal, where I had visited my brother a year previously, had said to me that I would be sent to Borstal if I didn't watch out. I said. You must be joking. I was sent to Borstal just as he said I would be for confessing to this crime. We were charged with malicious wounding.

On reflection I think my brother was not being a good brother to me. He should not have let me do it, that is let me take the rap.

Bubble Car Blows Up

During the time we were awaiting our court appearance we went one night to Bedford in the bubble car. On the way home the bobble car caught light and blew up as the petrol tank was above the engine. We managed to walk to Woburn Green and decided we would have to sleep the night there. After routing through some ones garage we found an old mattress and blankets and there was a newly piled mound of grass on the village green. This was where we made our bed and it was very comfortable. We put up our umbrella that we had rescued from the bubble car and slept soundly until the morning. The police, who wanted to know what we were doing - as if they could not see, woke us up. When we explained the bubble car had blown up they said oh yes they had seen it up the road. So they let us go without any further questions. I arrived at work that morning but was soon to be dismissed because I was due to appear in court and they were not prepared to trust me any more. This was the last of the bubble car as once we got it towed home my parents were able to sell it when we were in prison.

I Get The Sack

Once my boss Mr Sale found out I had been caught by the police he gave me the sack and so I had no job and was about to appear in court on charges of malicious wounding and carrying a fire arm without a license. So in revenge I had a plan. I knew where the money and the takings of the shop were stored over night.

Plan A Break In

So shortly after this I instructed my apprentice, Pat Jones, to break into the shop where I used to work and had been given the sack, and take the money.

The Break In

His task was to climb on top of the garage roof, lift the tiles off the roof of the shop and break through into the loft, and then the ceiling. Go into the rear toilet and take the money. A great plan so we thought.

The Shop

Sale And Mellor Shop Front And Rear

Then only trouble was that the money bag had not been placed in the spot that I instructed Pat to go to. So he did the job, did not get caught but we got no money.

12 Canterbury Prison

When my brother appeared in the Kent Quarter Sessions court I pleaded guilty to the charges of malicious wounding and carrying a fire arm without a license and my brother pleaded not guilty on all accounts.

The Fire Arm

The Offending Weapon

Canterbury Prison Together

I was sentenced to Borstal Training, which meant I could do any time between 6 months to two years. That would depend on me to some degree on how I behaved.

My brother was detained in custody until he appeared in court a month later during, which time we were both detained in Canterbury prison. Our time in Canterbury Prison was in one sense a time of continuous fun and just another of our good times together, even though I had just received an awful sentence.

Our time at Canterbury came to and end when my brother was found guilty and was sentence to two years prison at the Kent Crown Court.

I was a witness at his trial and was detained in the cells below the courtroom. When my brother was brought below, handcuffed to a prison officer, I was shocked and disappointed that he had been found guilty. In fact all our plans had come to nothing and I was to do a stretch in Borstal. He was found guilty of malicious wounding as well and was sentenced to 2-years in prison.

All Screws Were Bastards

On that occasion my mother was not allowed to see either of us and we were taken from the cells in Kent back to Canterbury prison that dark wet night. As we approached the prison gate I saw my mum with tears in her eyes out side the prison gate. We both waved and motioned to the prison officer to say she had come to see us and his reaction was, "So what, she can't see you because you are now prisoners". She had not got a visiting permit. She had travelled from Kent to Canterbury late that night to try and see us but she was rejected.

From that time we hated that prison officer called Titmouse. He was about 6 foot 7 inches tall. We began to feel from that time all screws were bastards. My brother, weeks later, after we were separated laid into this screw because of the hatred that had been bred in us by this screw. He head-butted him (nutted) knocking him out. Michael became the Ace of Spades, and of course was on a governor's report and put in solitary confinement. This I heard through the grape vine when I was at Wormwood scrubs awaiting my allocation to Dover Borstal.

Upon arrival at Canterbury Prison we were taken into the reception hall. Here we were with other newly sentenced young persons and being with my brother made it that much easier for me, and it gave me confidence because he had been to Rochester Borstal, and detention centre on two occasions before and he knew the ropes.

Canterbury Prison

This housed convicted and prisoners on remand and these were persons who were typical of the criminal population of England, at the time.

In this prison we shared our experiences with others who had been sentenced to three, four and six months, and many had already been to approved schools, detention centres and Borstal before. Some were on their second or even third visit to prison. There was an element of excitement and curiosity about what made people like they were?

In the reception hall we were issued with prison clothing. Our fingerprints were taken and photographed and we were each given a number. After this the medical officer (all prison officers were called screws) had inspected us and we were taken to our cell (called a Peter).

At that time we were three's up. My brother and I and a lad from Liverpool. In this cell we were to remain for a few days until we were issued work. The cell was approximately 12 foot by 9 foot and housed a bunk bed and a single bed. A table, chair, water jug and urinal pot.

Canterbury Prison

Canterbury Prison Gates

At half past six each morning our sleep was broken with a bang on the door and words saying "Slop out". This meant we had to get up make up our beds and empty the urinal pot. We then could get hot water for a wash in a jug for a shave and return to our cell. A razor blade was issued and collected after and then we were banged up until breakfast.

At breakfast time we were unlocked and had to line up in single file to collect our food. This was served up on a specially shaped metal tray, which was recessed in three places to retain the food.

Porridge For Breakfast

A typical breakfast would be a scoop of porridge, four slices of bread, a knob of margarine, a sausage or piece of bacon with beans and a large mug of tea.

The bread dipped in porridge became one of my favourite meals but on one occasion this practice of dipping bread in my porridge offended one inmate (when I was in Dover Borstal) he expressed he thought what I was doing was a disgusting habit. I just ignored him with contempt.

One of the ways we past time, when locked up in the cell, was to play "Blind Mans Buff". One of us would be blindfolded whilst the other two crept about and hid from the other, while the blind man tried to catch the others. There were all sorts of places to hide in such a small cell. We enjoyed this game we would jump from bed to bed which made the game that much more fun.

During this time I found time killing boring so I tried to read one ore two books. The books I found I could read were James Bond as these were about my level and the Beano and Dandy comics. Any other reading would be too difficult for me as I was virtually illiterate.

Moved to Different Cells

Initially Michael and I were in the same cell, with the lad from Liverpool but then were then transferred to different cells. I was transferred to a cell with two other people while Michael into a cell on his own. He hated being on his own so we agreed that I would swop places with him so didn't have to spend all his time on his own. I didn't mind a solitary cell.

In the cell that I was transferred too there were two older prisoners, and one of them had mercilessly tormented the previous inmate the had shared the cell with them. He had in fact tied him up, put his feet in the wash bowl, and set light to him. He was transferred out of that cell for his own safety. I was transferred to this cell.

I had to save myself from such bullying and this is how it occurred. On one occasion, when the evening tea was being served, I had to retaliate to a threat. This response to a threat helped prevent me from being bullied.

What happened was that the inmate whose job it was to was serve tea, came with one of the screws to our cell and poured the tea into my cup. Every one in the prison knew who this prisoner was. He was in fact a Fair Ground boxer and had a reputation that ensured that no one messed with him. Men would enter the boxing ring, at the fair, and try to win a few rounds with the champion, in order to win money. This man was the fair ground champion.

Well on this occasion he either deliberately or accidentally spilt the tea, as he poured it, and it missed my cup, so I simply said sorry. He in retaliation looked at me and fiercely said watch out. Well I was feeling low, and felt this response was unacceptable to me, so I turned on him and said he had better watch out as I was not prepared to put up with that kind of talk. He just looked at me, gone out. I don't think any one had spoken to him like that. Well that stopped any further intimidation and I was able to survive by my wits.

On the days we were not working, each morning and afternoon was exercise. This was where all the inmates walked as a body around the prison yard. No doubt each prisoner looked at the high walls and every building looking for a possible way to escape. During this time we could talk with whom we pleased, those that attempted an escape were made to wear yellow patches, so they could be spotted easily. These times became a time of communication and formed the prison grape vine

Hair Style Change

On one occasion I decided to change my hairstyle. So during

the wash period my brother removed the safety edge from the Government Issue razor and was able to shave my head. It was much easier to wash in the mornings with no hair and much fresher. However I had gone against the prison rules and was put on a Governors report and put in solitary confinement for a period of time.

At the meal time it cause an amusing stir and I was to get laughed at when one of the cooks slapped a handful of strawberry jam on my baldhead. After this when my hair grew a little I was able to razor a parting in my hair which was really the beginning of the hair fashions for the skin head.

What Sentence Have You Got?

I could not help but notice the various characters and the first points of conversation were "What sentence had you got and what was your crime, or crimes ?". After this an inquiry would be made as to your previous convictions and prison sentencing.

Wormwood Scrubs

I was moved from Canterbury Prison to Wormwood Scrubs in London, which was a Borstal allocation centre. After a period of four weeks it was decided I was to go to Dover Borstal. A closed Borstal called the Citadel. For the first time I was on my own and was moved from one cell to another having to share some times with others. I did not really enjoy things here, as it was lonely being on my own.

Dover Borstal (The Citadel)

We were allowed to go to church on a Sunday, which I did to break the monotony. How ever I remember when I was in Wormwood Scrubs I was horrified by the fact that I saw some inmate tearing a page out of the bible to role a cigarette. This was probably the first sense of me acknowledging the existence or fear of God.

The Scubs

Wormwood Scrubs

News Via The Grape Vine

Whilst in the Scrubs I heard news of Michael, from an inmate who also came from Canterbury prison. I was told Michael had taken his revenge on one of the Screws called Titmouse. It was this screw who had been unsympathetic to our mum when she had travelled all the way, from Kent Quarter Sessions court, to Canterbury Prison to see us, that rainy night. He showed no concern for our mum.

This screw was over 6 feet tall and intimidated inmates. Well Michael was not prepared to put up with him any more, and one day he head butted him and knocked him out . Of course he was put in solitary and dealt with by the system. This was the kind of news that travel quickly via the prison grape vine, from prison to prison.

How To Deal With Bullying

When at Dover Borstal I was placed in an open dormitory with five other lads. Here I had to learn to survive. There was a 6 foot 6 inch Lad nicked named Te Oh who was bullied mercilessly, by a 5 foot 6 spectacled, bottle job, called Vince Bowker. I saw this bullying the moment I arrived and Te oh was made to do this, do that, and he would say yes Vince, no Vince and so on. Hoping to get off lightly and an easy life. This went on for weeks and I felt sorry for Te oh. In the end Te oh turned and lashed out at Vice Bowker in anger and threaten to it him. That put stopped to that. I was determined I was not going to let that happen to me. I stood my own ground whenever I sensed any one trying to bully me. I was in fact nick named Flash Clarke because I acted as though I owned the place and I had all kinds of goodies like, cocoa, coffee, milk and sugar and even Ovaltine and had one of the Senior Green Ties (an inmate getting ready for release) make me Ovaltine in the morning.

Borstal Boy

Film Clip from Scum

This is a film made about life in Borstal featuring Ray Winston. This is a real to life story here ins the link Borstal Boy.

Scum this is a classic movie (Click here to view)

One bully, 6 footer, was moved into our dormitory because he had mercilessly bullied another inmate, who in fact was a married man. He had asked for solitary confinement to get away from being bullied, so the screws decided to put this lad in with me. We got on well until I one morning I decided to have a joke with him. I tied his shoelaces together for a joke, but he didn't see it that way. When he realized who it was that did it he was in a raging temper and he threw these tied shoes at me in anger. They hit me and gave me a black eye. The he came at me As he came at me to hit me. I was quick enough to take a defensive position and I to hit him right on the jaw. That knocked him down to the ground. After that he kept out of my way and the screws could see my black eye I had but just ignored it. I think they must have known how to deal with bullies.

Dover Borstal

Dover Borstal (The Citadel)

Electrical Installation Course

Whilst at Dover I went on a six months training course doing Electrical Installations and I worked really hard obtaining top marks every week and I use to be rewarded half an ounce of tobacco for coming top of the class. I traded this with an inmate for his ration of milk each morning and cornflakes and an egg each Sunday morning. We had to attend church on a Sunday and were would be marched to church in whatever the weather. We would have to be dressed in our best gear after Sunday morning inspection. I remember I had no sense of respect for God or anything like that. In fact when the vicar Rev. Whally took us for talks before we were to leave Borstal I can remember ridiculing him in front of all the inmates. I thought it was a huge joke.

Paternity Suite

Whilst serving my time in Borstal I was served with a summoned to appear in court to answer a paternity suit. A former girl friend was pregnant and I presume the Social Services had made her declare whom the father of the child was in order to get the finances but I am not sure as I never spoke to her about it. In fact I do not remember knowing any thing about it until I had to appear in court. The first time in court I admitted I was the father because I could have been even though I knew she had been with other men. At the time. I was ordered to pay maintenance out of my three shillings and six pence a week, at the rate if one shilling and three pence per week. I had no idea of the serious nature of being a father or bringing up children or any idea of taking responsibility for my actions.

My mother how ever was very anxious and after listening to the evidence given by the girl, she maintained it was not possible for me to be the father, as the timing of the events did not fit. She encouraged me to appeal and she really fought the case for me. This I did and with the aid of a Solicitor the girl had to prove I was the father of the child. When I look back it must have been humiliating for the girl because she had to explain when and where these events took place. My defence solicitor asked where the event or events took place. With incredulity he questioned her how could things take place in a bubble car, in the daylight. This I think on reflection was humiliating for her.

The suit was not proven and I was released from the charge. My probation officer Mr Moorland Hughes asked me many years later, when I became a Christian and had to appear in court over my confessions to many crimes, "Was I the father of the child", I replied I might have been.

The child was called David and my mother say's he had ginger hair. She had seen him out with his mother in Aylesbury whilst I was still in Borstal. He must be around 33 years old now.

I met all kinds of lads here in Borstal, car thieves, burglars, forgers, and gamblers. None of us had any idea for the reason of our existence but were probably looking for the best in life never finding it.

When I was released I was determined to have a good time. I wanted the best clothes, a good car, a speedboat, and a caravan. You name it I wanted all these things and intended to obtain them by one means or another. I had learned many criminal ways and had no intention going straight. I just had no intention of getting caught at any crime I may choose to be involved in.

13 My Release From Borstal

I was released from Borstal a year later and it was during this time I began to get into all kinds of things and criminal activities in Aylesbury.

My Gold Mini

My First Car 850 Cc Mini

I bought my first real car for £100 when I came out of Borstal. It was a gold mini 850 cc.

Home Leave From Borstal

About 6 weeks before I was released from Borstal I was given home leave and the first thing I did was meet up with some of my former friends who knew both Michael and I. David King and Brian Collier both took me out that week and we went to Berkhampstead to a Dance, during that week. It was there that we saw **Long John Baldry**, who had a hit record at the time, Let the heart aches begin. The trouble was he tried to sing it at the Dance without the orchestra and just tape recording backing track. It was not very good at all.

Returning to Aylesbury

When I had been released from Borstal I felt very cocky and was not prepared to take any nonsense from anyone. On my first visit to the Queens head, low and behold, Alan Dodd was there and he was with the girl (Liz Brown) who had taken me to court over the illegitimate child. We greeted each other and he realised, from the way I spoke I had just been released from Borstal because every other sentence of mine was peppered with, you know what I mean, or, do you know what I mean.

When we went to the toilet he came too and referred to the incident of the paternity suite and said he aught to hit me for it but let just keep things as they were as he was now in a relationship with the Liz Brown.

A Suit Made

It was at this time I went to the Crombie Shop, just off Kingsbury Square and had a Mohair suit made to measure but to my disappointment it never fitted properly despite may tries by the manage to have it altered to fit me. When Michael came out of prison he decided we should visit this shop and deal with the manager Terry. I talk about this later.

Government Training Centre Enfield

When I was sentence to Borstal I was assessed, in terms of my intellectual abilities, so that I would be sent to the most suitable Borstal. I wanted to train as a television engineer but the education department deemed me not intellectual enough, as I was poor at maths and English being virtual illiterate. So they sent me sent to a Borstal that offered Electrical Installations, which was a craft course not needing too much intellectual abilities. On this note, I talk from experience and now my qualifications, that Dyslexic people are very astute and can understand electronic so don't be put down or off by those who think other wise. I understood electronics, how circuits worked even though I could not really read or write.

It was due to my mothers insistence and tenacity that she managed me to get on the course at Enfield even though I was three months late. They thought I was not clever enough. I very pleased that I proved her right and came top of the group, in everything I did, in terms of practical work and the City and Guilds examination. It also confirmed by believed that Government officials sucked.

I Build A 4 Valve Superhet Radio

The first project I built on the course as a 4 valve superhet Medium Wave Radio. This worked great and every one in the group were impressed by my work.

Seventh Day Adventist

On this course I met a West Indian student , in his 30's, who was a Seventh Day Adventist, and he believed it wrong to eat pork. He argued that we must keep the Law of Moses, in terms of eating certain foods and the seventh day Sabbath, which was a Saturday. He put to me an argument that although fruits are fruits a banana in not an orange, nor an apple a banana but they are all fruits. So although days of the week are the same kind as they are all days, only one is the Sabbath. I understood his argument and agreed with him and at the week end, in Aylesbury I would put these things to Mrs Knight who was a Christian and worshipped on a Sunday, the first day of the week. She was unable to answer the argument. It didn't matter to me as I didn't care about such things but I felt my student colleague was more right in his approach and more s reasonable. I learned later that the Old Testament Sabbath was only a shadow of the rest we have in Christ. Every day to the Christian is the Sabbath.

I Visit Michael In Maidstone Prison

I decided to visit my brother who was now in Maidstone Prison and I did this when I could. Whilst he was there he met an inmate, a senior man from Cyprus, who told him some fantastic story, which we both believed. We had ideas of being involved in gold smuggling.

Maidstone Prison

Maidstone Prison Where Michael Was Sent

Escape From Prison

Michael was fed up with prison and wanted to escape so this opportunity to leave the country and smuggle gold was his opportunity.

Smuggling Gold

Michael was due out on home leave and instead of going back to prison voluntarily he absconding. The Cypriot was offering us the opportunity to make money by smuggling gold. The idea was that we were to pair up with a Cypriot girl and pretend to be newly wed. Then return to the UK on a honeymoon. We would both be carrying gold strapped to our bodies. There were no metal detectors or X ray scanners at the airports in those days. We would have a suitable partner and we would carry the gold strapped under our clothes making out we were newly weds. This would reduce the chances of being stopped by customs and so get the gold through. We were prepared to take the risk. It sounded exciting and that was what I wanted.

The plan was that when my brother came out on home leave we would go to Greece. We had to a contact in London all set up by the Greek man and take it from there. We were all hyped up but there was no such person or arrangements and we felt really let down. The gold smuggling came to nothing so Michael was on the run from the law for a year.

However my Michael decided he could not face going back to prison so he just did not return. He changed his name to Kenny? And managed to stay away from the police for a whole year before being picked up whilst working on a building site in Aylesbury.

I Am Not Me I'm My Brother

Michaels new identity enabled him to live work and take up normal life in Aylesbury and he by now had a steady girl friend which really helped to keep him on the straight and narrow.

How ever, one night while he was in the Crown Pub, in Aylesbury, with his girl friend, Paddy Dun, the local CID suspected he had identified the escaped convict. To verify his suspicion he called out hi Michael. But Michael realised what was happening ignored the salutation. Paddy then walked up to Michael and said, hi Michael. Michael simply turned round and said no I am David, I'm not my brother. This worked and Michael continued his life of freedom for a whole 14 months, living working and keeping out of trouble with the Police. You see the girl friend did the trick.

At this time I was doing a Government training course in Enfield Middlesex and Michael got some work with a shop fitting company and worked in London. He decided he would live above the shop, which was near Kings Cross, where they were working and so I was able to visit him during the week.

For a bit of fun one morning we decided to go to the cafe down the road dressing in our pyjamas and dressing gowns. Bringing with us our own cornflakes. We went into the shop and asked for breakfast bowls and milk and sugar. This seemed a funny thing to do and it all went down well.

Michael soon got fed up being there on his own so he decided he was leaving.

So one night we stole all the companies tools and equipment and returned to Aylesbury where our parents lived.

During this time I renewed friendship with Pat Jones and we did many things together. My brother had got a girlfriend now and I was seeking to have a good time.

Chloroform and its Effects

On one occasion I showed Pat Jones the powerful effect of chloroform and knocked him out so he was unconscious. Moved by my strange sense of humour I cut several chunks of hair from his head and when he came too he had no idea what I had done. I found it great fun when I took him home and saw his mother's face. Of course he had no idea what she was upset about. I just left and got out of the way laughing to my self.

It was after this that Pat Jones got the first skinhead hair cut in Aylesbury. No one would normally cut all their hair off it just was not yet fashionable. He did it and I was proud of him. I am sure he set the trend of the Skinhead fashion.

Mods, Skinheads, Greasers at Yarmouth

On one bank holiday weekend in 1969, when I was working for Radio Rentals in Hemel Hempstead, Pat Jones and I decided to go to Yarmouth and meet with the Aylesbury Mods, later called skinheads.

I took my firms Ford van in which we would sleep the night. On this particular weekend I was sleeping in the back of the Ford van that Sunday afternoon and Pat Jones was out with some of the lads. They had a run in with a crowd of Greasers.

Greasers were motor bikers who would fight with knives and motorbike chains. It was a very similar to the Mods and rockers you see in The Who film Quadraphenia. They were the sworn enemies of skinheads.

Mods On A Bank Holiday Weekend

Mods at Margate And News Reports

This company of Greasers had come across Pat Jones and his crowd when out on the sea front in Yarmouth and they were combing the area for skinheads, to pick a fight with. There were too many of them and Pat Jones and the crowd was on the run and I was happily asleep in the back of the van quite safe. Or I would have been had not Pat Jones came running up to the van shouting and screaming to get out and run, or do some thing. He ran off just having just called attention to these Greasers. As I looked up and came too and looked out of the van window I could see a crowd of Greasers grinning and running towards the van. They knew they now had a victim in a van. I was concerned it was the firms van so had to get away. There wasn't much I could do so I locked the doors quickly and jumped into the driver's seat hoping to drive. Unfortunately I was awkwardly parked. As I tried to start the engine a great whack came from the roof of the van. The van was hit a number of times with motorbike chains and I heard shouts of glee. Then they began to rock the van seeking to turn it over. They lifted it and rocked it as I tried to drive forward then backwards. I must have hit one or two as I managed to gut get away in time for a beating. That was all thanks to Pat Jones!

This how ever was all part of our fun getting into scrapes of one kind or another. On the way home that week end we decided to tow a four wheeled sea side bike back to Aylesbury so I got Pat Jones to ride the bike whilst we towed this bike all the way from Yarmouth to the outskirts of Norwich before deciding to lead it outside a pub as I began to realize we would be captured by the police going through London. It was all good fun and it made us laugh.

Newquay Here We Come

It was the summer of 1968, shortly after my brother had been released from prison and I had served time in Borstal. We had decided to go on a holiday. He had become friendly with a girl called Karen Mead but that did not stop our plans. We were going to go off with no plans to return. Michael had a nice long wheeled base Bedford van. This was fitted out with our equipment to live and we fitted a double mattress on the roof with a tarpaulin like tent. This was to be our sleeping arrangement. It was decided we would make our way to Newquay in Cornwall as I remembered going there with my parents when I was 16 years old. That year the sun was hot, the surfing was good and a really nice summer. We were off to seek the sun.

The Beatles Magical Mystery Tour

I had been to Newquay before and I told Michael all about it. It was the place to go for surfing and to seek the sun. The Beatles had been there before us and stayed at the Atlantic Hotel and were filming their notable film Magical Mystery Tour. The Beatles stayed at the

Atlantic Hotel in Newquay. They booked into The Atlantic Hotel in Newquay on Tuesday 12 September 1967 and left on Friday 15th. Newquay was a famous place to go on holiday and we knew why.

Our Bedford Van

This is where we slept for 6 weeks

The Atlantic Hotel Newquay

The Atlantic Hotel Where The Beatles Stayed

Our Holiday to Newquay the place of the Sun

Our first mischief that we planned but fail to do was the stealing of a speedboat, moored in the water at Barnstable. That evening we had planned to swim out to the boat and cut its moorings and float it down river to load on a trailer. That after noon we borrowed tools from a workshop and got some welding done to make a tow bar for the van. We needed a tow hitch to drive away with the stolen speedboat and trailer that night.

All went to plan until that night when we got the trailer ready but when we looked at the cold dark water, it being pitch black, we both lost our bottle and decided to call it off. We left Barnstable disappointed.

I Am A Waiter at the Gull Rock Hotel

Our first bit of work was to work in "The Gull Rock Hotel" in Newquay. I was a waiter and my brother was a kitchen porter. I had never been a waiter before but soon picked it up.

We were given sleeping quarters but we soon realized this kind of work and life was not what we wanted. The hours were unsociable hours. So the next morning we decided not to go to work, just stay in bed. We made a huge joke of it and expected to get the sack.

Sure enough we were knocked up when it was realized we were late but still we did not surface. When we decided to get up we went to the chef believing we had got the sack and so to collect or pay. To my surprise they hadn't sacked us but had just thought we had too much to drink the night before and were prepared to over look the sleep in. I said no we would leave and we each got the £1 each we had earned for the day's work.

In or mischief we went back to the sleeping quarters the next day where the girls were sleeping and jumped into bed with two of the girls. They didn't want this really and made a bit of a protest but before we left the manager's wife had been informed and came to see what was happening. As she came into the bedroom we were seen in bed with Angela the chambermaid. The manageress screamed, "Oh! Angela how could you". The girl got the sack and I felt really bad about that afterwards.

Shortly after this we decided to rob a petrol station to get some money. My brother tried to disguise him self by wearing a long girls wig but this made him stand out even more because he was flat chested and had no hips like a woman and this attracted attention rather than do the opposite. That idea was discarded so I decided I would take the money. When the attendant was looking after a motorist I crept up to the till and took the notes and ran away behind some building. Then quickly dressed in an old overall coat and then walked slowly away without being noticed.

We Return Home to Aylesbury

In the end I noticed my brother writing to his girl friend and somehow we decided to return home to Aylesbury.

After this I began to spend time with Pat Jones as my brother got more involved with his girl friend. Pat Jones and I got into all kinds of things, which I will mention later on. I was 20 years old and he was just 16 years so he began to learn many things off me, all which was probably bad for him.

It was after this I managed to get a job with Radio Rentals in Hemel Hempstead

This was a good job and at 20 years old I was the only Colour T.V. Engineer in the Hemel Hempstead branch and with a company car.

A Marriage In Gretna Green

Michael was in love with his girl friend but she was just 16 years old but her parents would not agree as he was on the run from prison. Not that they knew that, as he had change his identity and name. So Michael and Karen left for Gretna Green and planned to marry as soon as they could. This was because you could legally marry at the age of 16 with parents consent. How ever Karen got cold feet and ran away and their relationship ended after that event.

Michael then sold his house in Bracknel, moved to Spain, and lived a life in the sun on his Bob Cat Catamaran. This eventually got damaged in a hurricane and in 1974 I spent my summer holiday, helping him repair the ship in Denier Harbour.

Our Trip to Shoreham

About this time Ken Knight wanted to go sailing in Brighton so we agreed to go on the sailing trip to Shoreham near Brighton. This weekend we went sailing with Ken and Grace Knight. I took Mary Bilton, a girl friend of mine, Bernie Gilbert and Alison Knight and Pat Jones. Whilst we were there Mrs. (Grace) Knight went off to stay with a Christian friend in Brighton. Not that I knew that at the time I just thought she did not like sailing and it was a Sunday and she wanted to go to church.

The History of the Jews and 1967

A friend of Mrs Knight invited us back to this Christian mans home. He was called Tom and was a manager of an insurance company in Brighton. That afternoon he sat and talked to us all about the bible. I was almost convinced by his talk and began to believe there was more to the bible message than I had ever really liked to admit before. He told us about the history of the Jews and all future events. It was all foretold in the scripture. The history of Israel was recorded and the return of the Jews to the land of Israel in 1967 was clearly a sign of the last days. I have learned since then that such prophecy has already been fulfilled.

I was very impressed at what he said. So much so that I began to tell my friends at college the very next week all about it. This made me read parts in Deuteronomy about the curses that would come upon the Jews if they forsook Moses Law and reject the Lord Jesus Christ.

Pat Jones And The Bully

At this time Pat Jones was in his final year at school and he informed me of a bully who would relentlessly give him grief at school. The school was the Grange Secondary Modern School in Aylesbury. The school I had attended until June 1966.

One day at the evening youth club held at the school I decided we would sort this bully out so I instructed Pat " Bones" to do as I said. I was dressed in my long Crombie over coat, which my mum had altered for me, and inside I kept a large long heavy rubber torch, which was ideal for use as a cosh. Not too hard to break the skull and not too soft to do no harm. Just about right to knock some one on the head and possibly knock them out.

This was the plan. We were to go to the youth club and search out this bully. The Grange youth club was held behind the school buildings in some prefabricated buildings. It was early evening and not too dark and a few people were around. Here we looked out for the bully.

I gave Pat Jones the large heavy rubber torch and said to him when he sees the bully he must call out to him, " Come here" and walk towards him. When he came right up close he was to shout at him the words, " I have had enough of your nonsense and if you don't watch out I am going to set Dave Clarke on to you". He was then to point in the direction away from him so at to make him turn around and say' " look he is over there". When he turned around he was to hit him on the head, as hard as he could with the torch. Then say, " Now I am going to do it again and roar at him.

The plan went perfectly. We saw the bully dressed in a Denim Jean jacket he had slight ginger hair. I am sure his nickname was Ginger) and I had never met him before. Pat Jones shouted out to him and sure enough the bully came walking like a gorilla with his arms swinging by his side. Almost running to get at Pat Jones eager to get him. I was happy because this was where he was going to get the treatment. Pat did exactly as instructed. He said look over there and as he turned around Pat walloped this bully hard on the head. Every eye was on the two in conflict. The bully was stunned and his hands went up to his head to hold it as it hurt. Then Pat shouted at him to say he was going to give it to him again and sure enough the bully ran away as predicted. I encouraged Pat to chase after him to make sure he now knew his place. Every one looking on looked in amazement.

From that day forward Pat Jones had no more trouble from that bully. I felt quite satisfied in dealing this way with the bully.

How would Jesus have us deal with bullies today? This is a real problem to parents in a world of violence like to day. I was not a Christian but this remedy actually worked in Pat Jones's case.

14 Conversion from Crime to Christ

Having worked through and experience many things I often thought about life and its meaning. I could recall the absolute emptiness of my soul after going out for the evening and coming home. All was empty and what was the point to it all. I was seeking an answer to life, the universe and every thing.

A Bad LSD Trip

The following is an account, taken from memory and notes made of my experience of conversion to Jesus Christ on Friday, 16th January 1970.

Towards the end of 1969, I was continuing my studies at Luton

College, learning Radio and Television Servicing. We would often engage in discussions and it was quite easy to divert our lecturer onto subjects like spiritualism and the like. We would discuss what we would do if another world war came. We would talk about the future, as portrayed by Nostradamus, drugs and our experiences. At that time I was informed of a new film called **Easy Rider** and wanted to see it. On one occasion I obtained some hashish, mixed with opium and smoked this during our break time. This was so effectual I made use of the sick room at college to sleep and enjoy the illusionary effects of the drug, which amused my student friends.

On another occasion in January 1970 I had obtained 4 tablets of LSD from Peter Coppenhall, a student friend from Bedford, he was one of my fellow students at Luton College, and I decided to take them the following Friday night, 16th January 1970

On this Friday night Michael and I decided to take half a tablet each and Pat Jones had a quarter. He had been a close friend of mine (he was only just 16 years old) for some time and I use to think of him as my apprentice. I taught him all my bad ways. There was little we did not do together. I had known him whilst he was at school and encouraged him in crime, sniffing chloroform, smoking (marijuana, hashish, weed etc.) Drunkenness, violence and permissive sex. He was known amongst our friends as Bones, Patrick Bones.

My brother was going out that night with his girl friend Karen Mead so Pat Jones and I decided to walk up town and not risk driving for we did not know the effect this drug would have on us. I was dressed in my old clothes deliberately for I did not know what might happen too us. We tried to thumb a lift but eventually caught a bus and got off at the bottom of the High Street. As we walked past the pictures I noticed the film Easy Rider was being shown so we decided to go and see it.

The Film

Easy Rider Film

We wanted to take some one else with us, some one who was in their right state of mind, so we went up the billiard hall and found Bernie Gilbert and Mike Ellis but they said they would only come and watch the film with us if they too had some acid. I decided this was OK, and so we got a taxi back to my house to get the rest of the Acid. Bernie had half a tablet and Mike Ellis the other quarter. So all four of us were about to trip on acid whilst watching the film Easy Rider. We arrived back at the pictures about 8.45 P.M. and I fumbled a bit with my ticket as the acid had begun to take effect. Bernie and Mike suggested we go and sit up in the balcony but I thought to my self, what if we decide to jump off? I was tripping now and just followed them up the stairs. We sat two in front and two behind, but Mike and Bernie's trip had not yet begun as they acted and spoke normally.

I did not realize how tripped I was until the film had finished in fact the film records Peter Fonder and his friend actually on an LSD trip. During the film the acid had taken me on a very pleasant trip in time with the music. It was almost as if the film crew had deliberately filmed the film for me. They seemed to know how to give the correct lighting and sound effects. How ever Bernie and Mike seemed to be jumping about all over the place and it was irritating. I still was sitting in my seat when all the people had gone, before I decided there was nothing more to do. So we decided to up and go but Mike and Bernie were annoying me because they were mucking about.

All my thoughts and feelings began to reverberate four times over and thought patterns were being reflected and at the same time building and snowballing.

We walked outside the cinema and I said to the boys, Man you are all on the wrong scene you can't be turned on. Then I heard Mike and Bernie say he's turned into a wizard (Hippie) and there was a club room for wizards like me (The Dark Lantern Pub in Aylesbury). I then began a downward trip, which ended in the horrors. I began to feel paranoid thinking they were now sorry for me and were being polite in hiding their feelings from me.

As we went further up the road Mike Ellis asked if I wanted a scrap with some blokes across the street. It was as if he was testing me out to see if I was the same person he knew. I said no I didn't. I thought they had thought I had gone mad and they wanted to test me out. We went further up the high street and Bernie began to mess about and pull faces at me and make noises. I hid in a shop door way and told him to stop it and Pat Jones pulled Bernie away saying don't do it as he didn't understand. My horror began when I could not face the thought that they thought I had cracked up and gone mad. This feeling was too much for me to bare. More was to come.

We decided to go to the Crown pub and Brian Sale came up to me and spoke but I was out of my mind by now with this feeling of paranoia and could not speak sensibly and came out with a load of nonsense, so I had to say quickly I was drunk because I didn't think he would understand other wise.

I then saw Michael sitting with his girl friend and I went up to him and told him what was happening. He laughed and motioned to wined me up like a clockwork toy and then my mind began to distort so much so I had to run out of the pub to get away. Pat Jones followed me and I kept thinking the others were following us. I kept looking back as I didn't want them following me as they annoyed me. We left the Crown pub and walked towards Mount Street, via Richford's Hill and along Friarage Road. On the way down it seemed like a scene from a picture book and was like Alice in Wonderland with all the street lamps lit up.

The torment of my mind had grown so much that I could not bare the pain but I could not get rid of the torment. Ken and Grace Knight lived at Mount Street. We went down there with no real aim and as I arrived just outside their house Jock Macallion, another friend of mine, was about to leave and drive off. I jumped in besides him and told him my situation. After telling him I was tripped out of my mind I was thinking he would take me home and as I was about to ask him he said, Dave you are a worried man. I knew this and I now thought, so did every one else and being told that did not help me at all.

My mind was about to blow so I had to run again. I jumped out of the car and into 24 Mount Street where Ken and Grace were. I wanted to escape and so I told them my plight but I could not explain to them what was happening to me. Grace Knight recalled she thought I was in serious trouble and began to question me. This didn't help so I had to say forcefully I must have peace so they took me out to the summerhouse to lie down in peace.

No one seemed to understand the torment of mind I was in and no one could help me at all. I told Mrs Knight to leave me alone to work it out on my own and let me lie down. Then the torment got worse. I knew it was only the LSD doing it but I could do nothing about it. I would have to wait till it had taken its course. I thought it could be 12 hours or so but to me each moment seemed like an eternity of torment and I could not endure this any more.

I lay down and tried to settle my mind by thinking good thoughts and different things but my mind would not be controlled. The thought came, I may be driven to kill myself to get rid of the pain. I was horrified at the thought and the more I tried to stop thinking like it the more I thought about it. I looked around to see if there was a mirror or glass in the room and wanted to get rid of it just in case I cut my throat or wrists. I just did not know what to do I was at the end of my self.

In this condition it was evident I could not help myself. My friends could not help; my brother had not helped. Mr and Mrs Knight couldn't help, and I could not help myself.

In this desperation it came to me to call out to God for help. So I cried out calling on the Lords name saying, Jesus please help me. At that moment my mind went blank and his name appeared in the imagination of my mind but the torments soon came back again. I called out again and his name appeared twice and the happening repeated. I called four times in all and his name appeared four times and formed a square in complete emptiness.

I then began to feel emotional and wept but I didn't know why, and at that moment Mrs knight came to the chalet door to see if she could help. It was then, at that, a flood of guilt overcame me. I was convicted of the sin of adultery and did not know what to do. I beckoned to Mrs Knight to come in and said to her did she realize how bad I was and what I had done. I asked her to tell me the way what could I do.

Mrs Knight had spoken to me about Christian things and some how I knew she knew the way. Mrs Knight sat down and quoted the scripture saying, "For God so loved the world that he gave his only begotten son that who so ever believed on him should not perish but have everlasting life". (John 3 verse 16).

Dave I Am With You

After this Jesus spoke to me. I heard his voice, as clearly as I am writing this he said, "Dave I am with you. You have been searching for a long time, this is what our Father says, "What you have been going through is nothing compared to what hell is like". I replied with thanks giving saying thank you, Jesus thank you.

Mrs knight I thought that I was speaking to her she but she did not know what was going on.

It seemed that the words that Mrs Knight had spoken, were in fact the way out and pathway to my escape. It appeared as though I was at the bottom of a pyramid and the words were the way to the top and if I were to follow the words I would escape. I replied, thank you Jesus thank you.

I then thought of hell and my thoughts were about Pat Jones, Bernie Gilbert and Mike Ellis and I said what about the others. Jesus spoke again and said, all I could do was tell them.

I replied feeling it an impossible thing to do to convince them but, what more could I do? I was feeling the agony of the LSD horrors and knew I wanted to warn my friends of the hell to come. I reasoned within my self they will think I have gone mad on LSD how could I convince them, I wanted to do more than tell them. I asked what more could I do.

All I Could Do Was Tell Them

In order to answer my question the Lord took me back in time to show me all I could do was tell them. A number of weeks earlier I had reason to read about the curses that were to come on the children of Israel if they forsook their God. Deut. 28 v 53. "Though shall eat the fruit of thine own body". (I knew nothing about the back ground to these things) I thought it was saying people would be so hungry and having no food to eat a woman would be driven to eat her own after birth. Which of course was shocking. With this in mind these weeks earlier I was trying to shock this girl at work. I was working for Radio Rentals as a Colour T.V. engineer and I said to this receptionist how would she like to be so hungry to have to eat her own after birth? She responded with expected repulsion How could you say such a thing. I simply said I hadn't said it but God has. This thing repulsed her and she did not want to know anything about what I was saying (Not suppressing). However to this incident Jesus took me and asked me, what did the girl do when I spoke to her ? My answer was she shut her ears, as she did not want to know. It was repulsive to her. His reply was to me that, if I tell people about Hell and what I had learned and they screw their faces up and do not want to know I could do no more. The condition of the person listening is not my responsibility but theirs. All I could do was tell them. So tell them I would.

To these questions Mrs. Knight thought I was asking her, because I was speaking aloud, but before she could answer I had been answered directly from the Lord.

When Jesus stopped speaking I felt as though I was falling back into my torment and I prayed again, Please don't leave me. His reply was, I will never leave you.

Why Boast

Jesus then questioned me and asked me, Why boast ? This is because I was naturally prone to boasting among my friends, just to make a good impression. I reason within myself now and now knew I had no need to boast of anything. So from that day I have always avoided boasting.

My torment ceased from that time and the rest of the night passed with various thoughts going through my mind. Mrs Knight was not fully aware of what had taken place.

The next day was Saturday and I was due in to work but I decided to take the day off. I phone in to work briefly saying I was not up to work.

15 What after Salvation

Pat Jones had spent the night in the caravan parked at the side of the Knight's home, together with Paddy who had no where else to live. We spent that day together and I told them both of my experience. I assumed and expected them to fully understand and see what had happened.

Instinctively things were different with me. An internal change had come about and by it I had new desires. I no longer wished to live as I had lived and wished to be rid of my bad ways. No one told me I had to give up any particular way of life, I found within me an internal desire to choose the good and refuse the evil.

Evidence of the New birth

Upon reflection I say this was the evidence of the new birth and I later found this experience spoken of by the Lord Jesus Christ in Johns gospel. John 3. Jesus answered and said unto him, Verily, verily I say unto thee, except a man be born again, he cannot see the kingdom of God. The Apostle Paul also writes the same in Cor. 5 17. Therefore if any man were in Christ Jesus, he is a new creature: old things are past away; behold all things are become new.

I knew also there was a part of me which was just the same and when I would do good evil was also present with me. The Apostle Paul in Romans also expressed this. Rom. 7 verse 21. I find then a law that when I would do good evil is present with me.

Whilst this was my experience I found it impossible to convey this to my friends even thou I tried ever so hard.

What to do with Stolen Goods

I had in my possession much stolen property. In fact hundreds of pounds worth of stolen goods. I was no longer prepared to live off the benefits of stolen goods. What should I do? I had involved others in my crime of stealing and these could not help me now. In fact Mike West came to see me the next day and when he heard me explaining Jesus had spoken to me he began to fear I might go to the police and confess my crimes. I did not actually say to him I wanted him to return the Colour T.V. set, which I had stolen and swapped for his Citroen car but he was concerned, as he did not know what to think.

Poor Mike he must have panicked thinking I was about to go to the police, as he was concerned some of the stolen goods that I had left in his garage were a stolen including the mini engine sub chassis. I don't remember what happen to these parts but I asked Mike to dispose of them. I was later informed they had been dumped in the reservoir.

That Saturday evening both Pat and I decided to go to the Social Club at Park Street.

This was the usual thing for us to do on a Saturday night. I had determined to go and see my mates to explain what had happened to me. We walked down there but did not go in. After seeing one or two people I broke my news to them. I cannot remember what I said. I had no desire to stay so went back to the Knight's home. My inclination to live it up as normal was no longer with me. I now seemed at a loose end not knowing what next to do. From that time forward Pat Jones began to realize things had really changed for me.

The next day, being Sunday, Mrs Knight took both Pat Jones and I to the local Baptist Church in Southcourt, in the evening. I distinctly remember the passage of scripture the preacher spoke from. It was in Exodus where the whole nation of Israel was about to enter the Promised Land. However they listened to the evil reports of the 10 spies and did not take heed to the voice of the two good spies. Who gave encouragement to go in and possess the land? I remember also I saw, whether he preached this or not, that this was a picture of the body of Christ - the church of that day.

I Seek To Tell Others

After the meeting Mrs Knight introduced me to a Martin White who gave me a copy of the New Testament called the Good News for modern man. I began to read this straight away. This I received gratefully and began to read it every day as it was in simple English.

Southcourt Baptists

South Court Baptist Church

The following days were spent in the after glow and certainty of this new life that had opened up to me. I thirsted for knowledge, the knowledge of God in Jesus Christ. I told the folk at work about my experience and could not remain silent about the things I was learning.

My evenings were spent at Mrs Knight's home discussing the scripture with some of her Christian friends. Both Pat Jones and Paddy all seemed interested to hear.

My Own Ignorance, I Never Read The Bible

I am now amazed at my own ignorance then for until then I had never read the bible for myself. I did not know what the Acts of the Apostles meant. Within two weeks I had read the New Testament and thought I understood it all. I soon learned from the scripture that in the economy of Salvation it was the blood of Jesus Christ shed on the cross at Calvary that was the means of me obtaining a free pardon for all my sins. And also that I was given freely a righteousness to justify me before God.

In this respect the Lord Jesus was a true substitute and he died for me without cost at all to me. These were the things, which I learned and as it were drank in like water from the well of salvation. I learned them by reading the scripture and did not know them from the night Jesus spoke to me.

Difference at College

I attended college that week but there was a difference. I had decided I would not dress in my usual clothes to show off. Which would have been Levi jeans, white boots with red toe caps (or whatever colour I chose to spray them), a Ben Sherman shirt and loose leather jerkin. I felt I must not only be more sober but dress more soberly too i.e. Not show off as I use to do.

So I dressed in my best trousers, which were from my Prince of Wales cheque suit, shirt and normal pull over and normal shoes. Of course I had to tell all my friends about my experience. I protested to them look I even dress differently. They could not believe me. I told one of the lecturers, Mr. Jones, in front of them all but I was just given a smile of wonder.

I Tell Rupert

That same week I felt constrained to go and tell my friend Rupert, a West Indian from Jamaica. He lived in a room, at 14 Bicester Road Aylesbury so Pat Jones and I went to see him. As soon as I met him I told him what had happened in front of his new girl friend but Rupert's reply was, " I told you Dave not to take LSD ". Again they were none plus, they could not believe even though I tried my best to convince them.

Turning From The World

Being in the world but not of it. I did not wish to continue in the way of life that I had lived in the past. My back was now turned from the world that I once laid hold on, and had built for myself. I was self-seeking (ones own glory), asserting self without considering others, stealing, and thoughts of adultery, fornication, drug taking, drug selling, boasting, drunkenness, violence and worldly ambition. I say worldly ambition because I believe we all have worldly ambitions but when we are converted and come to Christ we are called to forsake it; that is forsake the world and its ambitions.

We all have our own worlds to forsake when we become a Christian. Some have a religious world to turn from; as a person may have been born in a religious family or have a circle of religious friends but in their world they have their own natural fallen nature to contend with. Fallen human nature seeks to gratify its desires and as such sin the whole day long. A religious person still has all the workings of a natural man as those who have no religion. Any thought or act, which is born out of selfishness, greed, pride, avarice, thinking evil of others, back biting, slander and prejudice may all be practiced by those in a religious or none religious world. So to forsake the world means to forsake all those thoughts and actions, which are natural to us, and are contrary to the way of Christ.

Religious And None Religious Persons
need to turn from their world

Some persons have no religion or religious friends, yet they too have natural desires and a fallen human nature, which they seek to please. Ambitions of fame for its own sake, the love of money, selfishness, the practice of gossip, evil speaking of others, are all to be turned from. It doesn't matter whether you be in a religious or none religious person we are to world are to be forsaken the world from which we come from, when we seek to follow Christ. We are called to be in the world but not of it. This is really what John Bunyan sought to express when he told his story of the man who turn his back on the city of destruction. One of the problems how ever was that his story only described the picture of those who were none religious and the pattern of their life styles. In reality a religious person, one who is not born again, has a pattern and life style, which is equally wrong and such need to be turned from. It is very easy for such a person to think because they do not do certain things that they see people in a none-religious world do, to look down and judge them thinking they are better than them. Not so, we all have a world to turn from. When a person is born again they have an ordinary life natural to them and are part of the natural world but we all must turn from our world in order to follow Christ

Being Kept By The Power And Grace Of God

I now had an inward and real desire not to continue in those ways, which I have just mentioned, for they just perpetuated my former sinful self, of which I had enough. A change of heart had taken place. This was the fight. That is not to say I could not be tempted to find pleasure in such sins there was a part of me still the same but I had a desire to put to death sinful thoughts and actions. Should I allow wrong affections to move me I was self-condemned with an accompanying self-abhorrence and I knew was not pleasing to God. By the grace of God I was able to resist and fight against sin.

What To Do With Stolen Goods

I was now moved by a new set of principles but here in lay a problem. I had erected a 48-foot by 24-foot wooden builder's shed on waste ground belonging to the Water Board next door to the Knight's home at 24 Mount Street. This became my garage and workshop. I had stolen the builders shed from a building sight in Berkhampstead. I had persuaded Mr. Knight to drive his lorry whilst me, Pat Jones and Paddy stole the shed panels from the building sight late one night by putting the panel on the back of our lorry.

The Stolen Shed

The Stolen Shed at Mount Street

In this shed was my newly acquired Citroen DS car, which had formally belonged to Mike West of Wendover. I had swapped it for a colour T.V. that we had stolen from old peoples home called Redlands, in Winslow. I had some lovely garage equipment which included a trailer, ark welder, trolley jack, air compressor, spray gun, tools, speed boat engines even a stolen car and various other items all of which by one means or another I had stolen or burgled.

My Citroen DS Car

What could or should I do now. I was responsible for at this stuff. Conscience would not permit me to continue to make us of all this stolen gear. What should I do? Should I just dispose of it all and brush the past behind me? How should I dispose of it if I decide to do so? I could not sell the goods for what would I do with the money. Conscience would not allow me to use it. I had in fact so much stolen property go through my hands, which had been disposed of by one means or another, none of it could be recovered anyway.

My Citroen Ds That I Acquired

Citroen DS except mine was Banana Yellow

I had only just stolen a nice new Mini car, which was about to be used to make me a lovely new car.

A Stolen Mini 1968

The body had been cut up and disposed of in my parents' garage in Finmere Crescent Aylesbury. (Whilst cutting up the body with the arc welder the hydrolastic suspension fluid caught light a nearly burnt the car and garage to pieces).

I had also another stolen Morris Minor Traveller, which I had swapped the number plates and disposed of the old body. This was and used it as a hire car. I think on reflection with hindsight and the faith I now have in God I would have been able to act differently than I did.

The Stolen Mini

My Stolen Mini

I was able during this time to return one or items of stolen goods. Late one wet night in February 1972 Pat Jones and I loaded the trolley jack into my firms van. I am not quite sure what Pat Jones thought about all this but I drove up to the garage from where I had originally stolen the trolley jack and parked on the forecourt.

Returning The Trolley Jack

The garage had been closed for the night (next to the Broad Leys pub on the Wendover Road, Aylesbury) and whilst no one was about I opened the van door and swiftly and quietly lifted the jack and placed it down on the forecourt. We then drove off as fast as we could. I often wondered what did the owner think when it was returned several months later.

I had no real advisers or any one who really knew the depths of my crimes and the amount of acquired stolen goods I had. I was faced with this problem what ever happens to me was no real concern but I did not feel I could involve others and get them into trouble.

The Broad Leys

The Broad Lees Wendover Road

Mike West was very fearful in case I confessed all to the police and he must have been puzzled by what was going on. I had hoped he would have offered me the colour T.V. back and I would have given him the Citroen back but he wished to keep the Colour T.V. so I gave him the Citroen any way, as I felt I could not use it.

Dealing With Sin And Temptation

I did not need anyone to tell me what was right and wrong. I knew the difference and in particular the sin of fornication. This is sexual activity out side of marriage. Sexual temptation was really fierce and strong to me, but by the grace of our Lord Jesus Christ I fought the fight against them. So much so that I had to avoid meeting girls because of a natural inclination, which had I given into would not have been good for them or me. The words of Jesus are clear that the very thought of sex with another mans wife was to commit the sin of adultery and I agreed. This area of my life was really difficult to me and would be to any new believer.

On The Love of God

It was common among Christians in my day to say smile God

loves you and enthusiastic people would wear badges saying smile God loves you. As though they felt this was the way to get people interested in the gospel, and to follow Christ. It was the time when Hippies were interested in love, and not war. And if you went to San Francisco you needed to wear flowers in your hair.

I however had read the scriptures and knew it was written Jacob have I loved, Esau have I hated. And in another place Pharaoh had been raised up as an object of God's hatred and he was destroyed. It was evident to me there was a lot of ignorance among professing Christians but I did not know how to convey the whole truth of God to people at that time. It would have been more accurate to wear a sticker saying God is angry with the wicked everyday and more effectual to make people think. The truth is that God loves the elect, those whom He had chosen in Christ before the foundation of the world. I could not reconcile how those who would be damned for their sins were ever loved by God.

Hippies in the Shed

Pat Jones began to acquire new friends and some were what we called hippies. They smoked pot, took drugs and generally did nothing but think about life etc. We invited them down to Mount Street as I felt it would be right to speak to them about Jesus Christ. About five or six came and they ended up sleeping in the shed.

Using The Stolen Shed at Mount Street

Whilst trying to speak the gospel to them I saw no real effect so I was disappointed. Perhaps one day I will see some fruit. I felt it OK to use the shed to house the hippies. About six lived in the shed for a number of weeks until they moved on. I thought I was putting it to good use.

My problems were solved by an intervention of God and his hand was clearly seen by all one year later.

This solution came by the knock on the door. It was the c.i.d who had come to arrest me for stealing the colour T.V. set that Mike West had and I had stolen from "Redfields" old peoples home in Winslow. This is where I started my story in the first Chapter of the book.

16 Going to Church

During the first few weeks of conversion unto Christ, in February 1970 there were a series of meetings held at Limes Avenue Baptist Church. The person speaking was Mr. Lance Pibworth and a girl called Geraldine Dunbar was being baptized.

Limes Avenue Baptist Church

Limes Avenue Baptist Church, Bedgrove Estate Aylesbury

I saw my first baptism here. After the meeting a man informed the congregation that if any one wanted to talk about any thing or ask questions they could stay behind.

Not Dressed For An Occasion

On this occasion I had brought Pat Jones and Paddy along to the meeting. I was dressed in my overalls and leather jacket, which I always wore when working on cars- I wasn't dressed up at all. I knew God did not look on the outward appearance but man may do so it did not bother me that we were not dressed for the occasion. I asked to see the minister Mr Sibthorpe and we three were invited into his study. I explained to Mr Sibthorpe about my conversion and wanted him to confirm that what I was saying to Pat Jones and Paddy was in fact true. On that occasion I half expected him to baptize me, there and then. I was under the impression, from reading the scripture, a minister of Christian were under direct command to baptize new believers as soon as they believed. I was very disappointed that he did not command me to be baptized that night. I knew nothing of church membership, modes of baptism, doctrinal distinctions and the like only that I should be baptized.

Shortly after this I met a man called Charley Tweedy, of the Church of Christ meeting (it is now a Seventh Day Adventist Church) at Stoke Mandeville Road, Aylesbury. He maintained that unless you are baptized you couldn't be saved.

He held some kind of responsible position in this Church so I explained to him about my conversion after which he gave me his telephone number to ring him if I needed too. I knew he was wrong about baptism but felt constrained to speak to him as I reasoned according to him, " I shall be damned if I die today if I am not baptized". I felt the need to reassure him that was not the case and he need not worry. When I rang him he seemed non plus nor moved with concern that I was not yet baptized. Again I was disappointed.

I Attend Various Churches

I had not been accustomed to go to any particular church but did go to a Sunday night meeting with Mrs. Knight. This was the Assemblies of God; Pentecostal church meeting at Rickford's Hill and Pastor Baker was the minister. Here I was received without any question and made to feel welcome. This was also the church Cyril Bryan went to and where I met Barry Crown.

The Church of God

This is where Charlie Tweedy attended Mandeville Road Aylesbury. It was here that I was informed that baptism by immersion was essential to salvation.

Church Of God

Stoke Mandeville Road

Rickford's Hill Assemblies of God

Richford's Hill, Assemblies of God Church Building

Giving A Testimony

On one occasion I was asked to give an up to date testimony as to the Lords dealing with me that week. So dressed as I was, in my working clothes (overalls) not knowing a difference between working days or Sabbath days, I went to the front of the congregation and gave a clear and detailed account as to how I had combated the devils suggestion to steel a car battery that week.

I had some trouble with my car battery and I needed a new one. The temptation was this. Here was I, passing Adam's Garage, on the Tring Road in need of a car battery. Just over the fence belonging to the garage were several car batteries. All I had to do was nip over the fence and help my self. This was the way I had thought in the past and would have done just that all one time. Not now. This kind of thinking was the old man of whom I had to continually combat and I knew Satan had a hand in the matter. To avoid this temptation I rebuked the devil and told him to clear off in Jesus name. On that occasion I told them the exact language I had used to the devil. I said to the devil, **"Bugger off Satan"**. I was quite unaware of the bad language I had used, and a number of years later Barry Crown remembered that Cyril Bryan gently reproved me for my speech. I did not know that I had said any thing amiss so was unaware that I had even been reproved for using bad language. I don't think I knew what the words meant any way.

I Am Baptized

I knew from the scripture and believed I should be baptized and I expected Pastor Baker of the Assemblies of God Church to command me to be baptized. I knew this was the command of Jesus and it signified the new birth, which I had already experienced. It also symbolized my union with the Lord Jesus Christ in his death and resurrection. That through his death I was to reckon myself dead to sin and my former sinful ways and that by his resurrection

I was to reckon myself risen with him to the newness of life, which is in him. No one spoke to me about being baptized.

At that time shortly after the Limes Avenue meetings I was taken to another group of Christians meeting at Fleet Street in a large shed. These were West Indians and the Pastor was Mr Bruce from Luton. This group also was having a series of meetings leading up to a baptism. I heard they had permission to use the baptistery at Limes Avenue Baptist Church so I asked Pastor Bruce to baptize me. He said he would and asked me to attend baptism classes that week with other people being baptized.

Fleet Street Pentecostal. Pastor Bruce from Luton was the overseer. I did not know what this was all about but presumed it was to make sure the person being baptized knew what it was all about. I was not told that after the baptism I was expected to join the church meeting at Fleet Street.

Fleet Street Pentecostal

Fleet Street Pentecostal Meeting Hall

I was baptized (dipped or immersed) upon the confession of my faith in the Lord Jesus Christ early one Sunday morning at 7.00

a.m. at Limes Avenue Baptist Church. My friends turned up, Pat Jones, Paddy, Paul Brooks, Mrs. Knight and Mrs. Chapski. Pastor Bruce baptized me in the name of the Father, Son and Holy Ghost, according to the command of our Lord Jesus Christ. Matth. 28 19.

Where Pastor Bruce, of the Assemblies of God Church, meeting at Fleet Street, Aylesbury, baptized me. I say this because I had met some that were teaching baptism was only valid if it was administered in the name of Jesus only. The reason being that they say the name of the Father is Jesus and the name of the Son is Jesus and the name of the Holy Spirit is Jesus. Gordon Smith, of Albert Street, informed me that some considered it was necessary to be re baptized in the name of Jesus only and that all other baptisms were invalid. I was not impressed by their reasoning and stress upon the singular name of Jesus to the exclusion of the Father and Spirit for Jesus had commanded baptism to be performed in the name of all three persons.

Mormons and Baptism

It was about this time that two Mormons spoke to me, whilst I was on the drive of our home in Finmere Crescent, and they were insisting that my baptism was invalid, as it was not conducted by a person having the right authority. As I had read the scripture and understood what baptism was all about, I realized that these men were wrong. In later years I came across similar views by some Primitive Baptists in the Philippines, but they too were wrong. I had been baptized, according to the terms of the lord Jesus, and that by immersion. My baptism was as valid as if John the Baptist had baptized me himself.

I knew that as far as I could discern from scripture, a man could be dipped, ducked, dragged, drenched, soaked, sprinkled or dribbled with 10 thousand gallons of water it would make not a scrap of difference to his spiritual state. Baptism could not affect the new birth, remove sin or make a natural man a spiritual man for that was the sole prerogative of Him that proceeded from the Father and was sent by the Son. John 15 26. The new birth being the effect not of the will of the flesh, nor of the will of man, but of God alone. John 1 13. Therefore Baptism could not save a sinner.

Baptism in the Spirit

I soon realized there were few churches in Aylesbury that believed the Baptism in the Holy Spirit was a distinct experience to being born again. I had no reason to doubt this and took it as a truth revealed in the Scripture.

I had no problem with this, as that was how I had read the bible. I actually felt I was baptized in the Spirit when I first believed and Jesus spoke to me. The only thing I seemed to lack was speaking in tongues. This had not happened.

I remember speaking to Mr Sibthorpe, the pastor of the Strict Baptist Church at Limes Avenue, about these things and he gave me an article written by John Stott who denied the Baptism in the Spirit, as I knew it. I was amazed at the way these people twisted and wriggled out of what God had plainly spoken about.

At that time I read as much as I could because this experience was not recognized by any other group of Christians apart from the Elim Pentecostal Churches. The best book that I read, at that time, was by Derek Prince called, "From Jordan to Pentecost". This gave a very clear and biblical position about speaking in tongues and it being the evidence of the baptism in the spirit.

The Christian Life

Being converted unto Christ was by no means an outward imposed principle I was not under a set of rules. I was not under any kind of legal fear to serve God. A rule, which says do this and you will be OK. There was no rest in works that I could do. . It was in fact the rule of faith. It was to walk by faith, without which it is impossible to please God.

I was what the scripture describes a "new man", with an inward desire to follow the Lord Jesus Christ. The scripture expressed these as God writing His laws upon the fleshly tablets of the heart Heb. 8. 10- 13. I began to read the bible straight away and I read the Good New bible within two weeks of receiving it, which was good going for me who could barely read. I was able to understand most of what I read and I thought I understood it all at first.

The Divine Nature Of Jesus Christ

Before this time I was ignorant of its contents and very soon the principal points of the gospel became very clear to me: The divine nature, or deity of Jesus Christ was essential to understand. Hell was real just as heaven was sure. The actual reality of Adam and Eve and the fall of our first parents. The need for the shed blood of Jesus Christ to remove sin. That salvation and the forgiveness of sins was by faith alone, without works done by us. We were not under the Law of Moses as the Jews were but under Christ Jesus' under his rule by His law the gospel of love and grace.

I remember trying to tell one of my friends about following Jesus saying that I didn't have to give up any thing to become a Christian. I simply found that I did not want to do certain things any more. It was not difficult. This lad came up to me sometime after this and I am sure he misunderstood me and in front of several other lads said, isn't it right Dave you don't have to give up any thing to be a Christian. He was expecting my answer to be no you can carry on just as you are. However I said that's right you don't have to give up any thing except sin. This silence him and I think they all got the point

Preaching Or Musical Entertainment

I learned that Gods way of saving people was through the preaching of Christ and him crucified. That the new birth was a must. What amazed me was the apparent lack of zeal and knowledge of them that had professed faith in Christ. Also how these persons tended to try and entertain people by means of music instead of preaching.

Giving my Testimony

On the 22nd May 1972 I was asked to give my testimony to a meeting of people in Luton to about 400 people. I was not sure what the meeting was all about so I simply spoke as I felt right to do. I spoke the gospel as best I could. I was not fully conversant with the doctrines of grace but I was soon to learn the word more perfectly. Providentially this meeting was recorded and may be viewed on:

Converted on LSD Trip 1972 David Clarke

(Click to view)

Every Day the Sabbath Day

Every day was the Lords day to me, as I awoke I was conscious of the presence of God and when I slept, yea even in my dreams. I knew of no distinctions of days such as holy days or the Sabbath day for I knew these to be abolished or fulfilled in Christ. Jesus Christ being the sum and substance of all the Mosaic Sabbath. He was the body that cast the shadow of Moses Law. Col. 2 16-17.

Authorized Version of the Bible

At the Assemblies of God Church, at Richford's hill, we had a representative from the Trinitarian Bible Society speak. Mr Cyril Bryan confirmed his belief how important it was to use a good translation of the Bible. It was pointed out to me that the modern versions often left out or changed the texts of scripture, which clearly taught the deity of Christ. From that time I began to be cautious of new versions and was happy to stick with the Authorized Version.

This was helpful because all the books that I had begun to read quoted from the Authorized Version and not modern translations.

Giving Money

On another occasion I was attending the evangelical meetings at Fleet Street Pentecostal church and there was an appeal for money to support the young musicians. The man making the appeal was so moving I felt I ought to give all I could. I reached to my pocket and put in the collection plate all that I had. I was giving as unto the Lord. I was given to believe it was for the Lords work and it was needed. I was happy to give. Shortly after this the same steward who had collected the money came back to me from the front of the meeting hall speaking and motioning to me with the roll of notes in his hand saying was I aware how much I had given. I said yes it was OK. It was probably about £200 as I was still use to carrying that sort of money around with me (1970).

Shortly after this at another meeting there was a visiting evangelist and he too made similar moving appeals for money. I had also spoken to him about the tattoo on my arm. This was because I regretted having it. He had been saying if I believed God then it would go by a miracle. I asked him would he pray to have it removed. At the same meeting he appealed for money with a prophecy saying the Lord had told him that each one had to go to their bank tomorrow and draw 10 per cent of all their money and give it to his fund the next day. It followed by another vision of an accident that was going to take place if it was not done. At the same meeting he said there was some one in the meeting that doubted God and they must get of their seat and come forward that if they did not then another warning was issued. I knew because of our previous talk he had me in mind. I then began to think his so called prophecy and visions were not of God but generated to control and manoeuvre people like witchcraft. I then opposed this and would have nothing more to do with it.

I even went to Mr Eric Connet and informed him that this type of talk and action was not genuine. Mr Connet was a preacher at the church and had some influence and could have helped to correct error.

I write this for the sake of any that may feel similar pressure from them who say that God sends them. Not all that is spoken in the name of Jesus is of God.

The Lord loves the cheerful giver. The Lord does not need our money. He wants our hearts. All that we have is His when this is the case. We are stewards of all that we own. I learned like the Sabbath there is no Sabbath day for every day is Sabbath, so with money there is no tithe of 10 percent but all our possessions are the Lords, not just 10 percent.

Sunday Cloths And Judging By Appearance

I was informed by my friend that the ministers son of the Pentecostal Church wondered at my being Christian. The reason being I some times went to church in my overalls and boots. It did not matter to me how I dressed in that sense but I was to learn that many people judge a person by the outward appearance and not the internal man.

Doing The Work Of An Evangelist

I found it my natural desire to preach and speak about Jesus to who ever I could. I remember working on a car in Mount Street one Sunday morning and a crowd of street kids all who I knew were playing around doing nothing. I was dressed in my overalls and leather jacket and I suggested they come with me to church. I decided to take them to a former Brethren Assembly called Granville Street Evangelical. I knew all these lads and realized we were all untidily dressed and that we may not be readily accepted. I knew however the scripture, which taught when you are invited to a meal, then take the lowest seat or place in the room. I decided we should adopt this principle so when we went into the hall, part way through the meeting. We slipped in and I beckoned them all to sit down on the floor. This we did without any noise. These lads were Paul Mitchell, Clifford Atley (Tatty), Michael Clark and one or two others.

Granville Street Evangelical

A Former Brethren Assembly

This is where I took the lads from the street to the meeting one Sunday morning. All the eyes of the congregation seemed to be on me. The meeting was stopped and a man came up and sure enough according to the scripture we were invited to sit on chairs towards the front of the meeting room.

Later on in that meeting they had what was called the "breaking of bread". They were an open communion church and their custom was to allow any believer to partake of the bread and wine. As the bread and the cup passed by they could help themselves. This bread and wine spoke of the death of Jesus till he come again. On this occasion however when the plate and cup came to our row it was passed by. We were judged as ineligible. I felt upset at this, as the stewards had judged us by an outward appearance and not as God. The problem then I suppose, **"I did not dress as a Christian"**.

I Meet Peter Howe Minister Of The Gospel

It was at this time I met Mr Peter Howe, a former pastor at Hearne Bay Evangelical Church, who also befriended my friends Paul and Sue Aston. Paul was a bible student studying at Watford and valued any help he could get. It was soon after this that Mr Peter Howe became the Pastor of the Ivanhoe Particular Baptist Church and Paul and his wife became members.

I Was Told I Was A Hyper-Calvinist

Mr Howe made it clear to me he was against what he called **Hyper Calvinism**, which he stated was the position of the Gospel **Standard Baptists**. It was not possible to make head way with him, as he seemed insistent that he was right. He was what is now called a **Fullerite Baptist**. He mocked the term "Dead Elect" a term that I understood to refer to the elect who were still dead in their trespasses and sins and had not yet been regenerated. I had no problem with this term and I had heard Mr Hill from Luton use this from time to time. I was classified by Peter Howe as a Hyper Calvinist.

Doctrinal Summery

By this time I had come to a fairly comprehensive knowledge if gospel truth. I had come to believe in the Sovereignty of God. The divinity of the Lord Jesus Christ and his eternal Son ship. The value and authority of the Authorized Version of the bible. The everlasting purposed of the trinity of persons in the Godhead, Predestination, Election, Justification by imputed righteousness and the new birth and a call to glorify God in declaring these things to others. And having knowledge of these things more than others enabled me to discern the many errors of many who too professed faith in Christ. I was shocked at the ignorance of so many.

I Hear Dr Martin Lloyd Jones Preach

I was encouraged by my friend to go to various Christian churches and on one occasion the church meeting at Long Crendon who had a visiting preached at their yearly anniversary service, he was Dr Martin Lloyd Jones.

Long Crendon Evangelical

Long Crendon Evangelical Church

This is where I heard Dr Martin Lloyd Jones preach This man had a real gift to preach and I could tell he understood doctrine, but he was never outspoken as to his belief in absolute predestination, although you could tell he would know these things and many more. I heard him also on another occasion as he preached also at the Ivanhoe Particular Baptist Church where Peter How had become the minister, and where Mr And Mrs Dix senior were members, along with Paul Aston and wife.

17 Getting a Job

This was a problem to me but I believed in God I knew that through the grace of our Lord Jesus Christ I would be provided for.

I had been sacked from Radio Rentals for stealing one of their colour Televisions from the old peoples home, in Winslow. It was the colour TV that Mike West had got. All I knew was how to fix televisions and I was qualified to City and Guilds 148. I decided to take the first Job offered me through the labour exchange; this was with a firm called Electroloid, in Aylesbury. I was being employed as a wireman and on the interview the foreman, called Dennis, asked why I had left my former job. I was determined to be honest so I explained I had been dismissed for theft. At this he asked no more questions and I was given the job. I was also able to negotiate for one day off, a week, without pay so I could finish off my college course.

I soon acquired a good knowledge of the equipment, which I wired up and began to read the circuit diagrams. My knowledge was such that I was able to fault find and develop test equipment.

Electroloid were a company involved in making equipment for electro plating and the particular equipment I was involved in was making was the controllers, for the automatic dipping of parts which required plating. A microprocessor would now replace the whole control unit.

I was soon asked to go out on site and trace faults on installed equipment. After six months I had been given the task of commissioning a controller in Southend. This involved doing what ever was necessary to get the new equipment operative. I spent a week away from home and successfully completed my task. I drew diagrams for the owner explaining how to fix things, if things went wrong. The owner of the firm was so pleased he invited me to apply for a job as their maintenance engineer. However I declined the invitation, as I was not ready to leave Aylesbury as I had just found Christian friends. On reflection I perhaps should have gone after the job as I now realise Christians are all around not just in Aylesbury.

Acting Foolishly

I began to get bored and impatient when I wasn't trouble shooting, which lead me to act foolishly. I began to experiment with charging lead acid car batteries and notice how the gasses were emitted from the battery when charged at a high rate of charge. During my tea break I decided I wanted to collect these Hydrogen Gasses, in a very large plastic bag. The size of this bag would cover an overcoat or suit of clothes. I then charged the battery at the rate of 50 A/H and soon the bag was filled with gas. I thought what would happen if this ignited so decided on a way to do it. I took two match heads and wrapped thin wire around them and then connected this to two long pieces of insulated wire. I hid behind a large metal cabinet and connected the wire to the car battery. This acted as the detonation. The "Bang" was so loud, the building shook and the whole factor stopped. The foreman came looking to see what had happened. I was so embarrassed I came out from behind the cabinet like a scolded dog with my tail between my legs. The manager, called Tom, asked what was happening. Before he spoke my conscience slew me if felt a fool and had dishonoured the Lord. I simple said the hydrogen from the car battery had ignite but all was well. I told my work colleagues all about it when they returned from break. I laughed about it but inwardly felt ashamed as I felt had let Jesus down because I had acted foolishly.

Boredom, pride and self-seeking became a snare to me and I soon began to joke and mess about at work and I felt unclean.

Working For Self

At that time my brother was out of work and Jock Macallion replacing windows on a council estate in Richmondsworth, had offered us work. So hastily I handed my notice in and my brother began to work together again. This work soon how ever came to an end but we soon found work in a building site as carpenters. We were paid £10 a day, which was good money and this, lasted a few weeks. One day on the site the men laughed at me when I told them about the Lord Jesus Christ. It didn't bother me but my brother, for the first time ever, stuck up for me and told them what I was saying was true.

Delivered From Fire, The Morgan Sports Car

After this we decided we would have to earn money at welding and spraying cars. I had the equipment and know how so we hired a barn, in Little Horward, and set up in business. It was cold at that time of the year in January and so we heated the workshop with an oil-burning stove called a "Salamander". We were supposed to use heating oil or paraffin but we used old engine oil.

This heater we called, "Sally the oil burning goose", because of the shape of the chimney. This was a dangerous heater as I shall now relate and I believed God delivered me from a catastrophe.

One day I had in the workshop a Morgan sports car, which was in for re spray. It was worth a £1000 (in 1972). I was working alone preparing this car with old Sally burning away merrily but she began to bubble and spit. This meant water was in the oil. Normally when this happened we shut her down and re-lit her but on this occasion she would not have it. She was so hot she erupted and oozed out gallons of hot engine oil, which flooded the floor. This went up in flames. The flames leapt up to the ceiling burning the polythene ceiling stretched across the rafters. The fumes and smoke and heat were so terrific. I cannot describe the event and terror I found my self in. What should I do? What could I do? All Alone in the middle of a field, in a wooden barn with, a pool of leaping flames just about to burn down the Barn and the Morgan car in side. My heart immediately motioned my soul to seek direct help from God. I had done all I could now I prayed aloud unto God for his intervention. I then left the barn with my back to it and my eye fell on an old damp tarpaulin, big enough to unfold and use as a fire blanket. In I went using the opened tarpaulin as a blanket and threw it over the burning pool. The flames were put out and smoke filled the place. The flames reappeared a few time but I soon put them out. God had answered my prayer and the flames were put out. The barn was saved and our equipment. Here God gave me the wisdom and courage and initiative to apply a natural remedy to my dilemma. God had saved me yet again. Praise God.

About 15 minutes later Mike West and his wife arrived and the knights for visit. They said I looked as white as a sheet. No wonder so I explained all that had happened. From that time Mr Knight inquired about getting insurance against such accidents but the insurance company refuse it on the grounds it was too risky.

Shortly after this I decided I would have to look for another kind of work.

I Find Work In Lowestoft

I found a job advertised in a national news paper working as a faultfinder at the Pye T.V. factory at Fleet, Lowestoft. This was in the summer of 1972. I decided to take the job. I moved into a Y.M.C.A. hostel leaving my home in Aylesbury and parents house. At the same time Ken took a job at the same factory and both he and his wife moved to Lowestoft for a short while. They eventually decided not to stay

Elim Pentecostal

I felt very lonely but soon got involved in the Elim Pentecostal Church in the town. Listed the local Christian bookshop and ordered a book called the Sovereignty of God by Arthur Pink. It was soon made known amongst the young people that I was a Calvinist because the mother, of one of the girls, served me in the shop. I found this out one evening when I was attending a young peoples occasion and the girl (about 20) said she thought I was a Calvinist, as I had bought this book from the bookshop. She then asked me directly saying was I a Calvinist. I said yes I believed in the sovereignty of God. She was the daughter of one of the senior members of the Elim Church. Her response was YUCK! And she turned around and walked away. I certainly felt hostility then. I decided I would speak to the elders of the church about some of the things I had learned but the idea of God choosing some and leaving others was not received very well. The thought of Particular Redemption was also rejected.

Whilst at the Y.M.C.A. I became very lonely and woke with a bad taste in my mouth. My mouth in fact tasted like the inside of a zoo keepers boot. This was a saying of Mike West. I decided to treat my self and ended up very ill. I began to take Andrew's liver salts and at first this was very refreshing. It was so good I began to take it all the time until one day at lunch I had stomach pains and when I tried to eat a salad then pain increased intensely. This set off a reaction, which lasted months and ended up me being treated for duodenal ulcers.

I remember speaking to one the workers at the Lowestoft factory about Jesus Christ. I had told him all have sinned and come short of Gods standard. He did not accept he was a sinner as he had lived a good life and loved football. He asked me how going to a football match could possibly be wrong, in the eyes of God and I gave a quick retort saying the scriptures say, "Go not with a crowd to do evil." I was thinking of the football hooligans but at that he said I was ridiculous.

In the summer holiday I returned to Aylesbury and decided to apply for a Job as a television service engineer in Tring and began to attend the Pentecostal Holiness Church in Bierton.

Working For Mr C J Ward And Son

When I arrived for the interview it was said, by Mr Ward, the owner, the reason why I had got the job was because I was on time exactly. I had not planned it that way; I just arrived at that time. I started work on the 14th August 1972. With a salary of £2000 per year. I was very thankful to God for His mercy to me.

I continued to work here and go to college at Luton to obtain a further endorsement on my **City and Guilds Certificate in Colour T.V. Servicing.** None of the people working here had time for Christian things in fact I was considered as less than nothing. I was ridiculed when I said, in the bible; God mentioned there was a Synagogue of Satan. They also treated the apprentice at a servant often humiliated him. I work here for 2 years but was not particularly happy there.

My Theological Training Dr John Gill

We always closed for lunch and it was during that time I spent each day reading Dr John Gill's, "A Body of Doctrinal and Practical Divinity", which I found so helpful and encouraging to read.

Michael Goes To Spain

At this time Michael had decided he wanted to live in Spain and so sold his house in Brackley and bought himself a Bobcat Catamaran. He lived in this boat in Denia and began to enjoy the delights of the Mediterranean sun.

Bobcat Catamaran

Michael's 8 metre Bobcat Catamaran

Michael difficulties did not stop however as it wasn't long before a hurricane hit the harbour in Denia and his Catamaran was dashed upon the rocks and one of the hulls was damaged. This happened however before the bad whether and he had invited mum and dad and me for a two week holiday. One side of the ship sank and after the hurricane cleared it was lifted out of the water with crane in order to repair the boat.

My Visit To Spain

My parents arrived and Michael found them accommodation on a friend boat and Michael collected me from Alacante Airport. I spent my first holiday from work helping Michael repairing the hull on his catamaran. On that tip I took with me Martin Luther's book, **The Bondage of the Will**, a translation from German into English by Erasus Middleton.

Pentecostal Holiness Church

When I returned to Aylesbury the summer of 1972 and got my

job with C J Ward and Son. I attended an opening service of the Pentecostal Holiness Church. A Rev. Gordon Hills was the preacher and was the pastor of the High Wycombe, Elim Pentecostal Church.

The Church Building

The Pentecostal Holiness Church Building

There was a series of meetings one-week and soon realised **he too was a Calvinist** as each night his theme in preaching was one of the five points of Calvinism: Total depravity, Unconditional election, Limited atonement, Irresistible grace, and Perseverance of the saints. I certainly felt encouraged and assumed Mr Harrison the minister of the Bierton Pentecostal Holiness Church were in agreement with these truths. At last I felt here was a place where truth and the Baptism in the Spirit went hand in hand. I was so encouraged.

I began to attend as a regular and got involved in the young people's work and very soon we had far to many kids from of the street to deal with. I was hopeless at discipline and how to control them. There was a wonderful opportunity but I found I was out of my depth and did not cope. Not only that but no one else knew how to cope either so the youth work was closed.

I was soon disappointed to find out Mr Harrison had no Idea about Calvinism or Arminianism and when I tentatively spoke to him about such issues he dismissed the whole subject as **"little issues of doctrine"**.

I began at that time to question many things and realised how easy it would be to be deceived if we were led by our feelings and not by the Word of God.

Do Not Be led By feelings

An example of this was shown to me when the pastor Mr Harrison informed the church that the Lord had shown him the bungalow, which he wanted him to have. This was in Windermere Close in Aylesbury. He said he knew it was the Lords will because he had offered the people a cut price and it was immediately accepted. This was the means, which Mr Harrison knew it was the Lords will.

The next thing the church was informed was that there were 17 clauses in the deed of purchase, which were unacceptable, and therefore the Lord did not want Mr Harrison to the buy the property. This was an example of what I mean, the Lord no more told Robert Harrison to buy the bungalow than he did to refrain from buying it. I did not feel or believe that was being led of the Holy Ghost.

Opposition To Imputed Righteouness

Mr Erice. Connet was another man whom I respected and he attended the Pentecostal Church at Bierton. One day in conversation with him, about the things of God and what I was reading and learning, he turned on me and said it was doctrinally wrong to say the righteousness of Christ was imputed to us for our Justification. This was because each one of us had to have a righteousness of our own. Jesus had his own righteousness for himself and we too needed our own righteousness.

I was shocked and on every occasion I could I sought to reason with him from scripture that what I spoke about was true I argued from the scripture that said, "As in Adam all die so in Christ shall

all be made alive". That as the sin and guilt of Adam (note: not the sin of Eve) that brought about the imputation and guilt of sin to the whole of humanity so the righteousness of Jesus - his life and death, brought about a righteousness that was imputed to all that believe. On this account only, do we have a right standing with God.

One Sunday morning he turned on me in anger and said all I did was talk about doctrine and never about the Lord.

I felt so wounded I just did not know what to do as I had always looked to this man for support and help. And I groaned in spirit feeling so alone in this situation. I wondered how should I handle this.

I Leave The Pentecostal Holiness Church

I was now unsettled at the Pentecostal Church over a few issues that I did not know how to deal with. When explaining to the minister, Mr Harrison, that I wanted to leave because they did not teach the doctrines of grace. He said I ought not to leave because of a little bit of doctrine being different. I found the issue with Mr Erice. Connet serious because he did not believe or teach that righteousness of **the Lord Jesus Christ was imputed to us for our Justification**. Although he had been a help to me he was one of the teachers in the church. Mr Harrison said he believe in the total depravity of man (not that he used these words) he said that there must have been a little bit of good, though ever so small in us for God to love us and want to save us. I knew that God set his love upon us and we had need of mercy and there was no good thing in us to recommend us to God. I also found the issue of being led by feelings rather that the Word of God very awkward.

The Three Day Week And My Redundancy

During this time I continued working for C J Ward and son until I was made redundant during the period of the three-day week in

1974. The letter came to me dated 8th February 1974. I was at home at the time of receiving this letter and its date was significant to me. I realised I was now unemployed. When I looked at the date I took courage, which helped fight the haunting fears of not being able to get a job because of my past criminal record. The Judge Col. Tetley, at the Aylesbury Magistrates Court, had given me a conditional discharge lasting for three years. This was on 9th February 1971. In other words my three years was up (three years to the day).

My Redundancy

From: CJ Ward & Son, 72 Western Road, Tring

8th February 1974

Dear David,

It is with deep distress the due to the present day economic position I greatly regret that we have to terminate your employment as from today week.

Rest assured this has no adverse reflection on your work or you present unfortunate illness, and will be more than pleased to give you any reference, which may be of help to you.

Should the economic position improve I would be pleased to consider any application you may wish to make at any time, and always pleased to see or help in any way possible.

Yours Sincerely,

C. J. Ward.

Enclosed P.45 and N.I. Card.

Please note we have sent off your National Health certificate and have not deducted any money from this on next week's remuneration.

My reference

The following reference was enclosed:

To whom it may concern

Mr David Clarke has been in our employ since August 1972 and has always proved himself to be industrious, courteous, and efficient and a reliable worker whom we have been pleased to have on our Staff. Since being with us he has taken advantage of Day College to obtain his City and Guilds endorsement, to add to his previous knowledge and certificates. We can thoroughly recommend him for any similar position and wish him well in such. We regret that the present government and country unrest and economic position led us, with great regret, to dispense with his services.

C. J. Ward.

My Response To Redundancy

I felt so encouraged by the date of the letter as it was 3 years to the day since I was given the conditional discharge from my Court case after the confession of my 24 crimes. Remember I was conditionally discharged on the 9th February 1971. It was as though my God and Father were saying to me don't worry I would take care of you. I could now look for work knowing and feeling I was free with a clean sheet to start from.

18 Working for Granada T.V. Rentals

I thanked God for within one week I was interviewed for a job at Granada T.V. Rentals and got the job. I started work for Granada T.V. Rentals Ltd. On 25/2/1974, being paid £37.27 per week. With a company car and £3.72 per week as vehicle allowance.

I found working for Granada a fresh breath of air and got on real well. And within 6 months I was promoted to workshop manager finding the work very challenging and rewarding. The only problem was I worked too hard and was inefficient.

Works Photograph

David at Granada T.V. Rentals

Michael Nicholson Phil Reason Tony Burnham Mrs Royce-Taylor

It was during this time I contacted Michael, of C J Ward, asking him if he wanted a job with Granada. He was the apprentice of C J Ward and whilst working for them he told me he wanted to leave as soon as he could. He was fed up with being treated second rate. He hated having to stub out the cigarette ends of John Ward in an ashtray. John Ward was the son of the Boss.

He came to Granada, past all the tests and he was accepted. He joined Granada as a Technician in October 1974.

My Visit To Northern Ireland

I was encouraged to have a break from work and in July 1974 I was invited by Owen Macrystal to visit his home in Northern Ireland, He lived in a town called Omagh in County Tyrone. Owen had a television business called, **"Crystal T.V."**. He started his business by bringing a van load of second hand T.V. sets from England to the town of Omagh and began to rent and repair washing machines and T.V.'s. I was invited out to teach one of his employee's, called Ivan. I taught him Colour T.V. theory. Owen maintained he was a genius as he could fix T.V. sets without knowing how they worked. He maintained any one could repair a T.V. set if they knew how they worked so he must be a genius as he could repair them not knowing how they worked. Owen's wife was a Catholic and I think they viewed my religious beliefs with scepticism.

I was unaware of all the conflicts in Ireland and completely ignorant. I had heard people speak evil of Ian Paisley and all I knew was that the Rev. Ian Paisley had preached this sermon called, "Second Mile Religion" and I knew from that sermon he was a man of God and preached the truth about the Lord Jesus Christ. I decided on my way through Belfast I would stop the night and visit the Martyrs Memorial Church where Ian Paisley was the pastor.

Martyr's Memorial In Belfast

Raven Hill Road

Meeting Dr Ian Paisley

When I arrived in Belfast I was amazed to see all the soldiers with guns checking every body and watching out for trouble. It was the 12th of July 1974. When I arrived on one of the streets in Belfast I noticed all the shops and doorways were barred up and the streets very clear with soldiers on every corner. I was unaware of what the 12th of July was all about. It was the end of the day and a lot of parades and marches had gone on that day. It was a day of celebration to some people. I ended knocking on a guest house door to find two ladies running this guest house. I had arrived unannounced with a large suspicious suit case in my hand from England. I said would like to stay the night and asked if they knew where Martyrs Memorial Church building was. They looked at me "gone out" and asked me what was an English man was doing visiting Belfast during all these troubles. I said I wanted to hear Ian Paisley preach. I said I had heard him preach on a record and he preached the gospel. They said they were Catholics and they would be too afraid to go and hear him preach even though they would like to. They made me welcome and I had a pleasant stay learning a bit about the troubles in Northern Ireland.

Suspicious Looking Suit Case

In the morning as I carried my suspicious looking suit case through the streets of Belfast I had occasion to as a milkman the way to Martyrs Memorial Church and he replied I was in the wrong part of Belfast to be asking directions to that place and directed me along a certain road. I realized this must have been a Catholic area but I was really so naive I did not know what was going on at all.

The Wrong Part of Belfast

I ended up in a Newspaper shop asking directions and my eye caught the picture of a man called "Carson", on a post card. To make conversation I asked the shopkeeper who was this person

Carson and she spoke scathingly to me say I ought not to ask such questions like that. I then realized I must have been in the wrong area.

I arrive at the Martyrs Memorial Church and Dr Paisley was preaching. It was a very large building with figureheads of the martyrs all around the building. Dr Paisley preached faithfully the truth about Jesus Christ and could not understand why people should oppose him like I had heard. In that meeting I heard no mention of politics I only heard about the Jesus Christ and what he had done for sinners. I concluded it must be his tone of voice or way of speaking I felt people must not be listening to his message but rather the tone of voice. I could imagine him speaking against the enemies of the truth using his tongue like a "Bastard file". After the meeting I asked Dr Paisley to direct me to some one who could help me get to Omagh, as I was a visitor. I finally got transport that day to Omar and ended up joining a group of Christians, from the Free Presbyterian Church in Omar. I was given an orange sash and joined their march along the streets and lanes of Omar. We then went to a meeting and the Preacher was Rev. William Macray.

I had a good time in Omar staying at my friend's home. Owen did not believe the gospel, he was a nominal Roman Catholic and we had long talks about the things of God. Ivan confided in me that he was a Christian but he did not like to say too much to Owen as it might not go down too well for him and Owen could give him a hard time.

The pace of life seems so much slower than that in Aylesbury and every one I spoke to seemed to have a knowledge as to what it means to be, "born again" or to "be saved". Even Owen and his wife, who were Catholics, knew these terms and used them. It was not like this in England. I had a good time in Ireland and would like to go again.

We Go To The Reformation Conference

A few years later my wife and I went to hear Dr Ian Paisley preach in London with our two children Isaac and Esther to a Reformation Conference, on 14th May 1983 in order to hear Dr Ian Paisley preach. At this meeting Isaac and Ether sat on Dr Ian Paisley knee and cried their eyes out as we took a photograph.

Dr Ian Paisley

Isaac And Esther Crying Their Eyes Out Tears Of Repentance

This meet we televised a may be viewed online at the following links. (Click below)

Dr Ian Paisley Preaches At Houndslow (click to view)

19 Mr Victor Prince
and the Crombie overcoat

In all thy ways acknowledge him and he shall direct thy paths.

The following extract is taken from my loose-leaf diary and relates to a remarkable experience, which demonstrates the wonder and way of the Spirit of God leading and teaching a believer.

On Friday, 30/8/74, it was my day off from work and during the day I was rebuilding our garage roof at 37 Finmere Crescent, Aylesbury. During the day I was thinking about the way God had dealt with me and led me thus far. I realized that each one that was child of God was special and God deal with personally. Each person had his own peculiar special work of God in his or her own life. A work done in no other and special to them. All were saved being involved in a common salvation but the work of God was peculiar and special to that individual. I this frame of mind I began to wonder about a particular trouble I had caused a Mr. Victor Prince.

Mr. Prince was a tailor and some years previously (about 5 years) I had employed him to make a Crombie over coat when I had just been released from Borstal. It was to cost £45 and I gave him £ 5 deposit to start the work. At that time I was living in London doing Government training course learning about Television servicing. My brother was due to be released from prison on home leave. He had a coat made by some one a year previously and on his home leave he came to see the coat before it was finished. After hearing how long it had been in the making he said it was taking fare too long and he persuaded me to tell Mr. Prince it was not good enough. He then picked holes in the coat in front of Mr. Price and told him to stick the coat. Later on the telephone we were both nasty to Mr.

Price. Mr. Prince thought I was saying I could not afford it and offered to keep it until I could. It was made especially for me and really would nod do any one else. I left it with Mr. Price and thought no more of it until then when I was on the garage roof.

I felt bad about the way I had treated him and would have apologized to him if I could.

My mind was thinking upon the subject of predestination and reasoned that God had planned every thing in creation to bring about a display of his glory and Grace in Jesus Christ. I was a person created by God being responsible and accountable to God having a definite purpose for my existence. I was alive and active but God was working in and through me. I had been predestined to obtain salvation by Jesus Christ. This work of salvation being the means of displaying Gods love, mercy and grace towards me. It was not my free will that saved me but Gods free grace that made me willing in the day of His power. Therefore glory was due to God the Father, Son and Holy Spirit.

Feeling wretched over the way I treated Mr. Prince I had resolved in my mind to pay the money I owed Mr. Price and apologies to him if ever I was to meet him again.

It was one week later on a Sunday the 8/09/74 that I saw the amazing hand of God at work. Mrs. Knight of Mount Street spoke to me on the way home from the Pentecostal Church at Bierton. She said her and Ken had met someone they had not seen for a long time. I stopped her speaking and told her it was Mr. Prince. She was amassed and wondered how I knew. They had meet Mr. Prince in Aylesbury and he had though of asking Ken to repair his T.V. as it had gone wrong. They said perhaps they would ask me to do it and if he remembered me. He certainly did. Mrs. Knight was able to inform him of me becoming a Christian and he left it to them to make arrangements to get his T.V. fixed.

I had not mentioned a thing to Mrs. Knight and there was no way of this happening by chance. God had done it.

The first Sunday after this we all went to visit Mr. Prince but he was out at a harvest a thanks-giving service at a Methodist church. So we made arrangement to go on 18th of September. At first I did not know what to say as I was extremely embarrassed so I said very little. I soon repaired the T.V. and then spoke to Mr. Prince about what had happened. I apologized and offer to pay the money I owed him quite forgetting about the coat.

It turned out he still had the coat even after several moves and the money owing was £38. All I was asked to pay was £34 so I paid this by cheque

(Cheque number 183901). I now had my new coat; it is dark blue hand made Crombie over coat.

20 Bierton Particular Baptists

At the same time of me working for Granada a friend who lived in Wendover, Mr Alan Benning, informed me that the Strict and Particular Baptist Church at Bierton, believed the doctrines of grace and that a Mr J Hill, a Gospel Standard minister (of Luton Ebenezer Church) was engaged to preach on an anniversary service, in the near future. I was keen to hear him preach. So I began to attend their weeknight prayer meeting.

Distinguishing Doctrines of Grace

My hopes had been raised that I would hear the truth about Gods free sovereign grace for it was reported that Mr. Hill was a Gospel Standard minister and was given to believe I would hear those truths preached by William Huntington, William Gadsby and John Kershaw. I had read their autobiographies and found their writings very helpful during my time at C. J. Ward and Son, and was encouraged by them as they gave all the praise and glory to

Jesus Christ the Lord and not to man.

I started to go the Bierton church just before Mr Hill preached that anniversary year on the Wednesday night prayer meeting, and sat at the back of the chapel. At that time I had no idea of the manor of service or church government nor of any other ministers engaged to preach on a Lords Day or weeknight service.

Bierton Baptist Chapel

Bierton Strict and Particular Baptists Chapel

I believed this same Jesus had called me by his grace directly and made him self-known to me outside the circles of any Christian church. It was he whom I sought and believed in when I went to hear Mr Hill preach at the Bierton Anniversary Service.

Mr Hill preached the distinguishing doctrines of grace very clearly. At that time I did not know many preachers preach these things except I had heard Dr Ian Paisley on a record and that sermon was called "Second Mile Religion".

I had also heard Dr Martin Lloyds Jones but he seamed not to emphasize the distinguishing doctrines of Grace although it was evident he believed in the sovereignty of God.

The churches I had attended until this time around Aylesbury and district appeared to only know of Arminianism and held to a false doctrine of universal love towards all mankind and a general atonement distinct from particular redemption.

Bierton Particular Baptists Articles of Religion

I felt lead and right to leave the Pentecostal Church and attend the Bierton Strict and Particular Baptist Church. I felt I could no longer in conscience stay or continue at the church even though I had affection for all the people there when there was a company of people across the road at the Bierton Strict and Particular Baptist Church. They held to and professed the very gospel I had received. From that time I commenced to attend as a member of the congregation at this cause of truth.

Denham's Hymns

The folk at Bierton used Denham's collection of hymns called "The Saint's Melody" and the substances of these hymns were very pleasing to me. Even the singing pace was different to all the other churches I had attended being that much slower.

Here Is A Sample Of The Bierton Hymns (click to listen)

Miss Bertha Ellis would play the foot-peddled organ and the hymnbook used was Denham's Collection 18 or 19 century. The hymn singing was about half the speed of the hymns sung at other churches and the words of the hymns were wonderful and glorified God. The stile of meeting was generally Hymn, reading from the scripture (Authorized version King James), Hymn, Prayer, hymn, Sermon, finally hymn and then a closing prayer. A short while after I began to attend on a regular basis I was asked by Mr. King if I would engage in prayer when asked too. It was the custom for men to pray the women would keep silent.

I did engage in prayer and after the meeting Mr King asked me kindly to pray in future in reverent language and address God in terms of thee and thou rather then you and your because it could offend people. That was there custom.

I went away feeling offended thinking all kinds of thoughts. I was upset thinking what difference does the language make etc. But I bowed to their request and adopted their form of speak in order not to offend. I now find it difficult, to day, to break from that habit of using thee and thou, I.e. Reverent language when addressing God.

The Bierton Society of Particular Baptists was formed as a Church in 1831, and this was the church that I became a member of in 1974.

The Doctrines Of The Gospel

I was convinced the Word of God was infallible and the only rule of conduct and religious practice. I believed the scripture taught us of a sovereign true and living God. That though God be one God, the only self existent being, one in essence and nature, there subsists in the divine essence three divine persons; The Father, Son and Holy Ghost. I believed that these persons were truly and properly God, by nature and that from all eternity. I believed that the divine nature was not divided but one in essence and each divine person possessing the whole of the divine essence.

I believed the scripture taught the Lord Jesus Christ is that only begotten son of the Father full of grace and truth, the only saviour of (Gods elect) lost sinners. He being one person yet having two natures. Being God from all eternity the divine Son of the Father and by nature truly God. Yet at the incarnation he took to himself that which he was not; our human nature and so was truly man.

Hence the glorious complex person of Jesus Christ is the Christ that should come into the world to save sinners. I believed that His glory was veiled during his time of humiliation.

This Jesus Had Called Me

I believed this same Jesus had called me by his grace directly and made him self-known to me, outside of the circles of any Christian church. It was he whom I sought and believed in when I went and heard Mr. Hill preach at the Bierton Anniversary Service.

Not all Preaching Was Good

Not all the preaching at Bierton was good as we had a range of visiting ministers. Some times I would groan and suffer 45 minute of difficult things to listen too. Very few were Gospel Standard ministers and some were opposed to the Gospel Standard position, they often liked to refer to the 1689 confession, a confession that I soon realized was in error. The Scottish Free Presbyterians Churches boasted of their 1646 confession as the best. Again I soon learned that this too was in error. Some of these preachers used notes whilst others did not. Not that, helped, as some I felt would have benefited from notes to preach. Some preachers would not use notes and speak as they felt lead too. But I realized that too was no guarantee they could be listened too.

Miss Ruth Ellis

She was one of our members and she was a gem of a person and always ready to share a word or hymn. On several occasion mid week we would visit her and she would read from her books stories about choice Christian experience.

Unfortunately Ruth died and she ended her days at Bethesda Home in Harpendon.

Mr and Mrs Gurney were members and their son John attended

our church as a member of the congregation. I noticed a plaque over the fireplace of their home and it read, "A Sabbath well spent brings a week of content but a Sabbath profaned, what err may be gained is a sure for runner of sorrow. I noticed this, as when I looked at the churches original trust deed there was no mention of Sabbath day keeping. It was only brought up in the spurious set of articles presented to me when seeking membership of the Church.

Miss Bertha Ellis

She was a mother in Israel and looked after most of the visiting ministers and played the organ at our meetings giving way to visiting people who were also able to play such as John Snuggs, Mr Dix from Ivanhoe

Miss Bertha Ellis informed me that the church was formed in 1831 and opened by the son of John Warburton. She had the minutes of that meeting which were signed in his own hand and the deed of trust upon which the church was formed. These articles of religion were very good and acceptable.

After my warm reception I was looking forward to hear Mr Hill of Luton preach at the anniversary service.

It was good to hear Mr Hill preached and he invited me and Alan Benning to his home in Luton and we spent time with him at his home.

My wife joins the Church at Bierton

At this time my wife Irene was received into membership of the church upon her confession of faith an acceptance of our Articles of religion as expressed in our trust deed of 1831.

Hats Or Head Coverings For Ladies

Trouble was on its way in the form of religious oppression. On Sunday morning in 1983 I took to church a friend of mine's daughter. This was the daughter of Dick Holmes who I use to work with as an aerial rigger. She had been through a divorce and was having a difficult time. I suggested she came with me to church, as she needed help from God.

She was dressed in tight black slacks and a short top, which showed all her figure. She had long peroxide blond hair and her face was made up. This mode of dress was a striking contrast to the elderly ladies who dressed very modestly with very little make up on and all ware hats to cover their heads in church.

Unfortunately this was too much for Mrs. Evered who came up to me after the service (I call it a meeting because the meetings of the New Testament churches were not called services) and she said to me the next time I bring a female to chapel I should tell her to wear a hat.

Mrs. Evered said that all Gospel Standard Churches insisted women cover their heads and so should we.

I responded that by saying, " what ever others do that was their concern they were wrong if they enforced the covering of the head upon a none church member and women visitor having no profession of the Christian faith."

I said she must raise this issue at our church meeting.

This spirit of legalism naturally took me back. Here was a young woman in severe distress needing the mercy and love of God as revealed in Jesus Christ and all Mrs. Evered seemed to be concerned with was the wearing of a Hat.

I knew the principle of a believing women dressing modestly and being in subjection to her own husband and covering her head in worship. I also knew the principle of the woman not exercising authority over the man or teaching a man but this action of Mrs Evered to use the phrase, "took the biscuit".

I was a man and was being instructed by a woman, Mrs Evered, to order or insist a visiting unbelieving female to wear a hat In order to uphold the principle that it was a shame for a woman to worship God without a head covering.

This covering according to the scripture was to show the angels she was in subjection to the man and not usurping authority over him.

Mrs. Evered missed the whole point of the gospel and in her religious zeal to maintaining an outward form of religion transgressed the rule she sought to maintain.

This religious spirit was not of God and I believed the gospel needed to be preached to set men free from such darkness. But who would do this?

21 A Call to Preach the Gospel

I believe God puts the desire to preach and speak His Word into the hearts of they whom he calls and gives the gift to preach. This desire was placed in my heart the day Jesus called me to hear him and believe in him. My desire to help others turn from the way that leads to hell and to Christ himself for salvation, was acknowledge by Jesus the night I got saved. His reply to me, when I asked what about the others, was all I could do was tell them. What better way than to preach the unsearchable riches of Christ to men.

I had spoken on a number of times at Bierton Church during the weeknight prayer meeting from the table not the pulpit. Gradually however I felt more and more uncomfortable when sitting in the pew just listening to sermons. Particularly when things were not very well expressed and some times serious errors were being spoken. It grieved me to listen to the ignorant talk off the religious whose eyes were blinded to the truth of God and who sought to bind burdens on peoples backs. This issue over the hat and lady visitor was an example. Not that I am against a head covering for a woman but what had happened to this lady visitor was wrong.

As I have already mentioned not all our visiting ministers were good at preaching and we were not a Gospel Standard cause.

I Did Not Believe In Bible Colleges

When I first became a Christian I did not believe in Bible Colleges. Thinking I did not want men to teach me, I wanted God to teach me. From what little I had seen of vicars and so called trained men I felt Bible Colleges were of no use because these people are not even born again.

Wolverhampton Polytechnic And Teacher Training

So I dismissed the idea of Bible college for me never the less I wanted to learn all about God and speak his word in clarity and truth. This desire turned me to read about the lives of men of God. I went from reading the Beano and Dandy comics and James Bond books to the Bible and then on to the writings of John Bunyan, Dr. John Gill, John Owen and Calvin in a matter of two or three years. It was when I met my wife to be that she encourage me to train to be a teacher and that is why I attended the Technical Training College in Wolverhampton, to learn how to teach technical subjects.

An Ulterior Motive

My ulterior motive was to learn how to teach the gospel. I took one year out from work and studied at Wolverhampton Polytechnic and finally graduated with a teaching Certificate in Education. This was awarded by Birmingham University in 1978.

I believed that I could learn from secular professional teachers how to teach and then would then be able to take the substance of what God was showing me and then present it to men in a way they could understand. This was my desire.

I took my first teaching post at Luton College of Higher Education commencing teaching in 1978.

Wolverhampton Teacher Training College

David (bottom centre right) at Wolverhampton Polytechnic

I Inform The Church Of My Felt Call To Preach

It was during this time at Luton College and at Bierton Church that I felt it right to make known my desire to the church as I believe I was being called by God to preach the word of Jesus Christ.

A meeting with Mr Hill and Mr Hope ministers of the Gospel

Mr. Hill of Luton and minister of the Gospel and Mr. Hope of Reading, minister of the Gospel invited me to share with them my calling.

Questioned About The Law Of Moses

Mr Hill questioned my belief regarding the Law of Moses and both he and Mr Hope listened. I expressed my understanding of the believers relationship to the Law of Moses and concluded the Law of Moses did not make the Lord Jesus righteous as he was always righteous. He had an essential righteouness independent of the Law. He did not have to fulfil the Law to become righteous. He always was righteous. Had he been judged according to the law he would have been declared righteous and so he was.

That imputed righteousness is the righteousness of God, given to all who believe, that Christ's Righteousness imputed justifies us, without our works according to the Law.

Mr Hill's Conclusion

Mr Hill concluded that my leading's were right and Mr Hope agreed. It was then put to the church that I should preach and exercise any gift I had. This was duly done and a number of people came from Albert Street Oxford and Eaton Bray church, to hear me preach the word of God that weeknight meeting at Bierton.

It was agreed without question that I should preach, as the Lord opened up the way, and from that day letters came from different churches asking me to preach at various Strict Baptist Chapels throughout the country. This was my being sent out to preach with the blessing of the church.

The Papal visit 1982

This year Pope John Paul 11 was due to visit Britain. This was to be the first time in 400 years.

Very few people saw the significance of this and I felt the need to inform people about such an event.

This year Pope John Paul 11 was due to visit Britain. This was to be the first time in 400 years.

Very few people saw the significance of this and I felt the need to inform people about such an event.

I wrote to the Bierton Church, which met on the 16th January

1982 (This was 14 years to the day of my conversion) asking if we could invite a member of The British Council of Protestant Christian Churches, Using the Bierton Chapel to meet and to teach clear biblical principles as to how we could act responsibly and maintain a Godly witness in the present time. I suggested it would be helpful to many churches in the area.

Mrs. E. Expressed the Bierton Chapel was not the place to hold such a meeting but some other place like the village hall. Mr. King said they had Roman Catholic friends and would not wish to offend them!

From this time I began to wonder about the church at Bierton and believed I would see the hand of God out against her.

I remembered, "They that honour me I will honour".

I held the meeting in my house and invited several people from different churches and Rev Gordon Ferguson came and preached for us.

Our Bierton Home

Our Home In Bierton. 187 Aylesbury Road In Bierton

Just a few minutes walk from our Bierton Chapel 187 Aylesbury Road. We eventually was able to by a property in Bierton it was a detached bungalow just down the road from the Bierton Strict Baptist Chapel. I felt really blessed by God to own it and being so near to our chapel.

A Spanking from the pulpit
(Isaac deserved it)

I was very conscious of the instruction that I was responsible to God for the discipline of my children and knew the scriptures, which speak of spoiling children through lack of discipline. And the exhortation that if I spare the rod of correction I would spoil the child (Prov. 13. 24). The other scripture, which spoke to me, was that of how a good father ought to " Rule his house well, his children being obedient and subject to him ". That if I did not know how to rule my own house how should I be able to take care of the church of God (1 Tim 3. 5 - 12. I believed the scripture spoke clearly about corporal punishment and it was a must. (Prov. 29. 15 and Prov. 23. 13).

The first occasion I felt the need to exercise corporal punishment was on Isaac when he was very small. As I write this now I smile and I am sure he would do too. I think he needs corporal punishment now at the age of 20 years old.

Isaac had done some thing, which warranted correction, and I felt this occasion I would use the rod of correction. I was a small thin garden cane, a green one. I made him stand away from me and I said it hurt me more than it would hurt him, to have to correct him like this. He was about 4 years old. I smacked his bottom with the cane and he jumped and couldn't say a word for a few moments. Then he burst into tears saying, " daddy that stings". From that day forward that cane was called the "stinging stick". That was not the last time the stinging stick was used.

On another occasion I was preaching in Bierton Chapel and Isaac and Esther were sitting with there mum on the back row of the chapel. During the sermon Isaac was playing his mum up and he would not sit still and kept messing about. His behaviour was unacceptable. I was gradually becoming cross with him until I felt I must do some thing about it.

I stopped speaking and said to the congregation " excuse me" and climbed down the pulpit steps and went to the back of the chapel. I picked Isaac up and took him out side the chapel and informed him I was displeased with his behaviour and gave his three smacks on the bottom. With this he burst into tears and when he stopped I took him back in the chapel and placed him besides his mum. I then went back into the pulpit and apologized for the interruption and proceeded with the sermon as though nothing had happened.

I heard afterwards the spanking was heard through out the chapel and a couple of the ladies were horrified at what I had done but they said nothing to me. I felt I had done the right thing using the rod of correction to drive foolishness from the child (prove. 22. 15).

Is Corporal punishment what Jesus wants?

Hatred stirs up strife's but love covereth all sins. (Prov. 10. 12)

Prov. 10 13. A rod is for the back of him that is void of understanding.

Prov. 13 24. He that spareth the rod hateth his son: he that loveth him chasteneth him betimes.

Prov. 19 18. Chasten thy son whilst there is hope spare not for his crying.

Prov. 19 29. Judgments are prepared for scorners and stripes for the back of fools.

Prov. 19 30. The blueness of a wound cleanseth away evil: so do stripes the inward parts of the belly.

Prov. 22. 15 Foolishness is bound up in the heart of the child but the rod of correction will drive it far from him.

Prov. 23. With hold not correction from the child: for If 13 - 14 thou beatest him with the rod he shall not die.

Prov. 29 15. The rod and reproof give wisdom: but a child left to himself bringeth his mother to shame.

Answer: Yes.

Preaching The Gospel

In a very short period of time I was engaged to preach at the following Strict Baptist Chapels throughout the country:

The Various Churches I Preached:

In fact I was so overwhelmed with being asked to preach at so many places, I could have been preaching three times on a Sunday every week of the year and during the week on weeknight services. This was on top of my full timework, which involved teaching two nights a week at Luton College as well as continuing my studies with the Open University.

Reading "Hope Chapel" Strict and Particular Baptist GS	Oxford "Hope" Chapel Strict and Particular Baptists GS
Wantage Strict and Particular Baptists GS	Stamford Strict and Particular Baptists GS
Oakington Strict and Particular Baptists	Horsham Strict and Particular
Fenstanton Strict and Particular Baptists GS	Romford Room Strict and Particular Baptists
Matfield Strict and Particular Baptists GS	Eaton Bray Strict and Particular Baptists GS
Walgrave Strict and Particular Baptists	Bradford Strict and Particular Baptists

Reading "Hope Chapel" Strict and Particular Baptist GS	Oxford "Hope" Chapel Strict and Particular Baptists GS
Beeches Road Strict and Particular Baptists	Evington Strict and Particular Baptists GS
Leicester "Zion" Strict and Particular Baptists	Nottinghamshire Strict and Particular Baptists
New Mill Baptists	Winslow Baptists
Black Heath Strict and Particular Baptists	Attleborough Strict and Particular Baptists

The Bierton Pulpit

David preaching at Bierton Strict and Particular Baptist Church, 5th June 1983 I Preach At Various Churches

22 I Go Fishing For Men

Front Page News

Former thief says: Come and be helped

REFORMED drug-taker and thief David Clarke hopes he can **pass on the secret which diverted him from a life of crime.**

For David — now a Christian and Baptist preacher — hopes his belief in the Bible will help his former friends to make more of their lives.

SERVICE

And he is planning a special service at 5.45 on June 5 to try to reach the people who were once his partners in crime.

David Clarke of Aylesbury Road, Bierton, was convicted of 23 crimes when he confessed to them after his conversion to Christianity on an LSD trip in 1971.

He claimed at his court hearing that Jesus spoke to him while he was under the influence of the drug, and has been determined to pass the message on ever since.

"It is now time I tried to spread the word to the people I used to know in Aylesbury when I was a teenager," he told us.

"There are still many of them left in the town, and they have gone through broken marriages, drug addiction and crime."

LECTURER

"I hope they will come to my service and see what Jesus has done for me," said David, who is now married with two children and lectures in electronics at Luton Technical College.

He returned to Aylesbury 2½ years ago to rebuild his life.

"My adolescence was spent taking all sorts of drugs and stealing. I am glad I saw the way out of that," added David.

The service will be held at the Street Baptist Church, Bierton, and he has thrown open the invitation to all his ex-drunkard, criminal and drug-taking friends in Aylesbury.

The Bucks Herald Thursday 19th May 1983. Price 8d.

Bierton Meeting 5th June 1983

In May 1983 I was engaged to preach at the church in Bierton on Sunday 5th June 1983. I have always had that desire to catch men for Jesus Christ but how do you do it. I was now living in Aylesbury and a lot of my former friends are still in and around Aylesbury, having no hope and without God in the world.

I felt compelled to do some thing to get the message of the love of God in Jesus Christ to them some how and tell them what Jesus had done for me and that I was preaching at Bierton Church I decided I should go and ask the Bucks Herald,a local news paper to give me some free advertising. I simple went to the Bucks Herald office and told them my story. I said I wanted to reach all my old friends to tell them what the Lord on, 5th of June that they were all welcome.

I was prepared to advertise but I know I was being cheeky in asking for it free. Little did I realize it but I was giving them their front-page news for the week. Before I knew it the photographer was out to see me and a reporter taking notes for a story. It all happened so quickly

The story appeared as follows on the front page of the Bucks Herald on Thursday, May 19th 1983.

Meeting Televised

Providentially this meeting was televised and can be viewed on Youtube at: Click the blue text.

David Preaching at Bierton Chapel 5th June 1983

A News Paper Report

I was landed with a problem as I did not expect any of this to happen and I hadn't informed the church and so I felt the need to explain what had happened in case it offended any one. I felt relieved when no one was upset.

I felt the need to be very careful because in October 1982 I had already found some opposition from one part of the church and I was not out cause trouble. They were against a certain good minister and visiting preacher because he had used the term Evangelical Repentance and that he read the Evangelical Times. I had defended this man in every way I knew how but for the sake of peace the church decided not to asked this man to preach again. I was very sad and disturbed by this and I believed from that time Satan was provoked by my actions. And there was more to come. So for this reason I felt the need to be extra careful.

The following week I went fishing, looking in the pubs, and visiting people's homes looking for my former friends in crime, in order to bring them along to hear what Jesus had done for me and could do for them.

It wasn't long before the national news network were on to me and wanted the story which I believe appeared in one of the national news papers. I was disappointed in the write up because I felt it was trivialising the reality of what was going on. This is the official transcript:

Dear David Here's what we put out on the national Telex service. Looking forward to seeing you at the service June 5th Yours Peter Game

From Peter Game, OX and Bucks NA Catch:

Service Reformed crook David Clarke is hot on the trail of his mates in crime. He's turned detective to trace thieves, drug pushers, burglars, bandits and drunks in a massive one man round-up aimed at changing their lives.

And it could result in the most bizarre meeting of shady characters a town has ever known.

David, 33 wants to pack them all into a tiny church at Bierton, bucks, and tell them how God saved him from spending a life behind bars.

And if the Local C.I.D. Force at nearby Aylesbury, bucks wants to turn up and join in the hymn singing too they are welcome. David a married man with two children from Aylesbury Road, Bierton, is a preacher in the Baptist church.

He said, "God helped me and can help all my old buddies too".

David an Electronics lecturer at a Polytechnic explained:

" I 've already persuaded some old villainous pals to come along. I want to pack the church with criminals, but it's going to be a tough job".

The former thief and drug user left Borstal aged 18 and decided to lead a life of luxury based on crime.

"I was in a car ringing business, thieving vehicles and knocking them out again," he confessed.

" I've broken into an old peoples home to steal a colour telly, taken garage equipment, nicked from tills, walked of with speed boat engines, and taken drugs. I've even sold drugs and got involved in permissive sex.

"There were times when I used to keep an axe and a mallet in my car just in case. Now it has all changed.

His life took a drastic change when he "met Jesus Christ" during a bad LSD trip and joined the Baptist Church.

And when detectives questioned him about an offence he did not commit he confessed to 24 he did carry out.

He Added " I've had a clean sheet for 13 years. I'm not going to preach the bible at the bad boys --- Just show them how God helped me and let them make up their minds".

Ends.

Memo to news desk: Service on June 5th. **We believe this man is absolutely genuine in his actions.**

Memo End.

Out Come Of The Meeting

The meeting went ahead as planned but not many people turned up. I heard that some did not come because they did not wish to be associated with each other. Pat Jones and Malcolm Kirkham were now enemies. Pat Jones had not long ago been around Malcolm's house to blast him with a shotgun. Malcolm had been involved in drug pushing and other things.

Mike West said he wasn't prepared to sit or be associated with drug pushers and criminal's etc.

My brother Michael and mother came but Michael did not appear to take things all that serious as he had brought with him a stocking to put over his head to pretend he was a burglar. See the video taken after the Bierton Meeting.

After the Bierton Meeting

(Click to View)

I had spoken as faithfully as I could of the Lord Jesus Christ and I remember saying from the pulpit how good God had been to me in blessing me with a good Job, a wife, a nice house, children being in church and many friends what more could a natural man want. I had comments made by several people that God had really blessed me providentially and I knew it.

Doctrinal Opposition

I was questioned after the meeting about my reference to the love of God and the point was that I had informed the congregation that the love of God is towards his elect, those who were chosen in Christ before the foundation of the world. This love knows no change and is the moving cause and why those chosen to salvation actually come to believe the gospel and be saved. They are loved with an everlasting love. The rest of mankind do not benefit or experience this salvation. This concept is know as Calvinism and was back bone of my actions. I knew through the preaching of Christ to men those chosen by the Father, redeemed by the Son would be called by the Spirit and be saved in due course.

On reflection it seems from this time I was battered from every way. First my church membership was lost, then my health, which affected my call to preach. Then my children were attacked, then my home was lost, and then my Job is lost. Then my faith in God was lost, which lead to me giving up on my marriage. I write about all these thing in my other book.

My Troubles Begin

As I write this it reminds me of the story of Job who was truly blessed by God in his own soul and in material things, then Satan came seeking to destroy his faith in God. God gave Satan leave to do it but the end of Job was blessed spiritually and materially better than his beginning. Thanks be to God. I hope my story will reflect the same faithfulness of God to me.

23 The Road Divides

Michael Goes To Thailand

Here I tell of my brother Michael's life and eventual imprisonment in the Philippines serving a 16 year sentence.

Michael Goes His Own Way

As mentioned already after the Bierton meeting, on the 5th June 1983, Michael did not really take what I had told the congregation very seriously. Never the less he continued his own life and began to prosper in business ignoring the things of God. His life had been unaffected. He becoming the Director of his own company **Tudor Charm Produce**s and **Penny Wise**. But life's difficulties hit him, which led to him experiencing depression, divorce and the loose of all his money. It was this experience that led him to do some thing different and start his life all over again.

It was then [1991/2], Michael started his own company making movies, in Thailand, called **"Paradise Movies"** and he involved our Mum and Dad, who lived in Eastbourne, to sort all his finances out whilst he was away. He also took Jessica, his 10-year-old daughter, with him for the summer, which cause her mum great alarm when he did not bring her back to England. He said at the time that he wanted to get back at his ex - wife because of all the grief she had given him in the past.

Thailand

Paradise Movies   **Paradise Express**

In the end Michael's business in Thailand went wrong. His equipment was stolen and he ran out of money. We don't really know what he got into while in Thailand but Mum was so fed up with bailing him out with money and favours that she finally said she had enough of him as he was making her ill. We later got news of some of his activity through a News of The World Article, I learned later, from Michael, that this story was a complete fabrication.

NEWS OF THE WORLD, January 19th, 1992

EXCLUSIVE by MARK CHRISTY

Michael The Pirate   **Michael The Policeman**

Sailors beware! A new nautical menace has appeared on the horizon - a con man Michael Clarke has set up a scam to keep himself supplied with booze and birds on a paradise beach.

He has ripped off scores of unsuspecting British yachting folk by offering them jobs in an epic sailing movie he claims is being made in Thailand.

Clarke's ad in Yachting Monthly magazine promises free return airfares and £40 a day for a five-day week. All he wants is a £55 insurance fee from applicants.

But there is No film and punters NEVER hear from him again.

Former Watford market trader Clarke reckons four square rigged sailing ships are going to be used in the movie 'Invasion of Thailand', set 200 years ago.

He calls himself Peter Timberlake and operates his con from the

"Paradise Suite" in the Thai City of Patiya.

But his "Office Suite" is a seat in one of Patiya's hundreds of girlie bars. And his firm "Paradise Movies" Inc. Does not exist - though he does have a home movie video camera in a local pawnshop.

The slogan of "Paradise Movies" is "A cut above the rest". And when the News of the World found Clarke he was half-cut above the rest.

An investigator confronted him at Jan's Bar. "Yes I am Paradise Movies", he slurred. "But I've been up boozing all night and need to think before I speak to you."

Then he vanished and our man found him at The Jasmine, on Patiya's beach, - a bar offering girls for sex. He was working for £2 per night touting for customers.

Asked if he intended to return the cash he had defrauded, he replied, " I can't even afford the price of a beer".

Thai Police and Immigration officials are now looking into the fraud.

One British yachtsman who fell for the con is architect Fred Howell of Christchurch, Dorset.

He sent off his £55 after seeing Clarke's ad in November, and even rang Thailand to check.

Mr Howell, 55, said, "someone there said they would look for him in his office, so I assumed it was genuine" .

Yacht skipper Alan Stevens of East London, also wrote but smelt a rat.

"When I contacted Yachting Monthly they admitted they had lots of complaints about the advert", said Alan, 47.

No one from Yachting Monthly was available to comment.

Michael Writes Home Seeking Help

Needless to say Michael got himself into trouble and wrote home to our Mum and Dad for help. This is Michael's letter home that he sent shortly after this news article.

Punnee Bar Babbua Muang, Kanchanaburi Thailand 7100

Dear Mum and Dad,

10/06/92

How are you both? Keeping well I hope. It will be good weather in England so you will be able to enjoy your garden. It's been four months since your last letter, which you sent to Peunnee Bar in Kanchanaburi. That was the only letter I ever received from there. I did reply to that letter but everyone seems to be having problems with mail to and from England.

Last time I wrote I was working for a tracking company but after I set them up with two main agents they double-crossed me. Things here are getting from bad to worse. Six weeks ago I lost all my money £700. I was in my room on a raft house. A big storm came, which caused a lot of damage, a lot of my belongings went to the bottom of the lake 100 meters deep, together with my money and Passport. I reported it to the police and got a report to give to the Embassy in Bangkok. I wrote to the Embassy in Bangkok but so far no answer. In my letter I told them I had a photocopy of my passport and lost my money. I am in Thailand with no money and my visa is out of date about £400. I also told them I had no one in England to help me financially. The tourist police told me not to worry, as it was an accident, which should stop me from going to prison. Now I don't know what to do. At the moment I am living with a Thai family 80 Km east of Kanchanaburi at Sisawats Great Lake. They have several bamboo raft houses designed for tourists but they are in very bad repair so I am helping them to repair them so at least I get food and keep (but no wages). If we get tourists I will get some money but at the moment it is low season and the many political problems in Bangkok is not helping. If I don't hear from the Embassy soon I will have to try to go to Bangkok to see them.

I Have Been Stupid I Was Never Happy

I know that over the past few years I have been stupid. I have lost every penny, even my daughter, and my credibility. I am stuck in Thailand penny less. Even if I could get home where would live and what would I do? I am not well and I am not young and most of all I have no spirit to live. Even when I had money I wasn't happy. I know I had a reasonable job and a nice flat but I was so screwed up inside it was sending me crazy. Even when Jessica came to see me it was heart breaking for me when she went home. I know you both love Jessica very much and because of me you cannot see her, I wrote to her a couple of times but no answer.

Please Mum and Dad give me a few words of wisdom as I think that this depression could be the end of me. I thought of writing to Brandon Gibson in Australia but I don't know his address. May be he could help me with some money and I could work to pay him back.

All my TV and video equipment you sent I lost due to massive tax duty and also a crook that tricked me.

The weather here is hot every day. It seems the same, just like England's heat waves when you get them, but the water in the lake is clear and fresh and night air is refreshing. Every one I speak too says the tourist trade in Thailand is finished.

Marriage Break Up A Cause

Please write to me soon and let me know how every one is. Even a quick word to Jessica to say I love her would be good for me. Please when you write don't give me a lecture on how irresponsible I have been and on how much you have helped me. I know all this and am truly sorry. My marriage break-up I think was the cause of it but I don't know.

I expect my financial situation is very bad at home and Margaret and Chris think I am very bad. Please what can I do now?

Well today is another day and I have just heard from the British Embassy. They tell me that they have no financial resources to help me even though I lost my money and passport. They say I must have money sent from England to clear my over - stay, about £400 otherwise I will be in prison without a doubt. So now it's making me ill and this Thai family cannot help me much longer. I have written to a few people in Thailand to see if they can help me with a job but I don't hold much hope.

I have heard that in Bangkok I could possibly get a job teaching English but I would have to go to Bangkok to check it out. At least if I could get my visa in order and it would keep me straight with immigration and stop me going to prison. The Embassy pointed out any money should come through Thomas Cook Travel Agents and send it to their head office in Siloam Road, Bangkok and would only take 24 hours or so and on proof of I. D. I could draw it. But I would have to know when to go to Bangkok, which would mean a telegram here first to let me know from you. I know you think I have a damn cheek after all you have done for me over the years but I have no one else to turn to. I have written to David and Irene for help and advice.

A Fear Of A Thai Prison

I really am going crazy with the thought of going to a Thai Prison.

If you cannot help I will understand as I feel that you have done too much for me in the past and I should be old enough to take care of my self, but this is Thailand in the 3rd World.

I have just had a thought ----- for me to get to Australia. I need a return ticket out to get an entry visa and this I doubt if Brandon would do anyway but please try and locate his address for me.

Please send my letter on to David, as I do not know his new address.

Write soon and take care.

Your loving son Michael.

P.S. I have written to the Embassy again asking what will happen if I give myself up. I think they will hand me over to immigration to lock me up. Then the Embassy will inform you that I am in Prison but I don't know.

Mum And Dad Fed Up With Michael

Mum and dad were fed up with what they thought were Michael's irresponsible ways and they despaired of him. I think mum in the end sent him the money to get him out and back to England.

On a letter received from Michael Mum wrote "turning point" so I assume she felt Michael was changing his ways.

Turning Point

Mum writes turning point on the top of a letter dated 10th July 1992, sent by Michael from Sam's Place, Song Kwan Rd, Kanchanabari. Michael writes, "Last week I went to Bangkok to speak with the embassy but they told me no help can be given what so ever and the only way is to get some money from home to clear my visa overstay and an air ticket home. They said they would get their office in London to contact you. I have also written to Auntie

Edith.

The straight facts are as follows: I have been on overstay since February 16th which is 100 B fine a day= £350 to date. And to clear it I must have the money to go to the immigration plus an air ticket home £300. If not I will go to prison and work off my fine for £2 per day. Then I have to pay for the air ticket and deportation costs, which doesn't get me anywhere. They will keep me in prison indefinitely until money comes. Every day I stay here is about another £2.40.

I am ill with worry. I do not have any thing left here or in England, only my family who have helped me time and time again. I have been so foolish over my life. I have no will power to go on living. I cannot face the future. I know I must find a way to get back to England. David said I could live with him for a while which could be good as I could not face living in Eastbourne. I would have to start where nobody knows me, as I can't handle being with people who know what's happened to me since I have been in Thailand.

Why did the Embassy tell you I was fit and well? How do they know how much I am suffering inside myself? At the moment I am living at the above address. My clothes I keep in a hold- all and I keep it in the toilet of a boat where I sleep on deck at night. I get food free but that's all.

Please, please help me, as I know the Embassy cannot. Please give me a ring with a word of encouragement. The best time is at 11 am your time. Just ask for Michael. PS. I have written to every one I know for help but no joy.

All my love Michael xxx.

Michael Returned To England

On Michael's return to the UK he came to live with me for a short period and it was then he began to work on his next project which was his idea of being a Travel Agent.

Michael and the Philippines

"Paradise Express" 1995

It was then he developed his ideas to form a travel business. He had met Freddie Laker earlier in his life and put together his business plan; **"Paradise Express"** and he informed me of what he intended to do in the Philippines, in February, 1995.

To keep this account short Michael got involved in arranging holidays for single men to take advantage of the easily available sex on offer by G.R.O's guest relations officers.

The rest of Michael's story is told in our joint book Trojan Warriors and the book, **The Rise And Fall Of Brother Bobby.**

ISBN 9780953947331 by Jeff DuBuisson

How ever I got news of his arrest on national TV in the UK when he appeared as headline news on ITN Television. I was shocked. And wondered what could be done to help.

24 Michael's Call for Help

Michael had written to me in 1998 asking me to help him and I could tell from his first letter he was in a very bad way. He told me of another Englishman, Suny Wilson, who had been "set up" for a crime he did not do and was sentenced to death in 1996. Michael use to visit him on Death Row and spend time together. The Philippine Supreme Court acquitted Suny Wilson, on the 19th December 1999 through the help of Alan C. Atkins and Errol Wilkinson and he had given Michael a small paperback entitled **"Mere Christianity"** by C.S. Lewis, on his release. Michael read this book and was later convinced that Jesus was the Christ the Son of the living God. Suny Wilson's Story is told in **"Sentenced To Death"** by Alan Atkins and Earl Wilkinson. It is also available as a Youtube Video:

Sentenced To Death Suny Wilson (click to view)

Michael's letter indicating a true change of mind and heart

Dear David,   7th May 1999

With regards to me writing my life story etc, for you to include in your book! Please David forgive me but I am so screwed up, I just could not handle it right now. It takes me all my strength to just write this letter to you...

I am so very pleased that you are concerned for me and that you include me in your prayers and your fellow Christians. I do believe in God and Jesus Christ but even though I pray and ask him to please forgive me, for all my sins, and to help me to be a better person and to take over the rest of my life on earth and to lead me into heaven - I do not want to go to hell because I know that what I am suffering now is nothing to the perpetual hell which would await me after physical death on earth. My faith is not strong enough and I am so very, very, confused.

Skinny And Withdrawn

Even if I get out of here what am I going to do with the rest of my life. I am looking very old, skinny, withdrawn. I have not smiled in almost 4 years. Where am I going to live? How can I earn a living in my condition?

Oh, David I am so very afraid of the future and it hurts me so much to even think about it. I have become old before my time and all I can see is loneliness in some dingy rented room and no chance of ever finding some one (a lady) to love and share things with. Oh, David what am I going to do?

The only thing that stops me thinking about suicide is that hell will be waiting for me and the torment there will be a million times worse. Will I ever smile again? Will I ever love again? Will any one love me again? Is it possible to be happy again? I do not have any reason to live and that is so very frightening. Oh, David I know you have your problems that may be greater than mine and to be honest I do not know how you cope. How do you manage to keep working and keep your home going, the loss of you wife must be absolutely unbearable? May be you can suggest how I tackle my problems of the future, for me there simply is no light at the end of the tunnel.

When I leave here I don't even have a pair of shoes. I will have to start all over again but the question is how do I start all over again? I simply have no will to live and I just could not cope with living on my own as I know I would not be able to fend for my self. To think of buying a property is really out of the question. What do I do? What do I do?

I Am Ashamed Of The Many Things I've Done

Another reason why I cannot think of writing my life story is because I am truly ashamed of many of the things I have done and I don't really want to broadcast my evil past for every one to read. I have confessed to the Lord and I just hope He will forgive me.

You asked me how I felt about you becoming a Christian 30 years ago. Well I was quite proud of you but felt you were a little over the top but I never mocked you in any way. My heart broke with Karen Mead and the collapse of Tudor Charm and my divorce I will expand on that some other time so please David not at the moment, you may have to wait until I am released.

At the moment I am taking each day at a time and I keep praying that I will be acquitted of this horrible conviction, which I hope will give me added strength to face the future. I am sorry my letter is so depressing, all I can do is pray to out the Lord for strength and guidance.

Once again David thank you again for not forsaking me and I am sure you will be always there to give me support.

Please give all my love to the Children Regards Michael.

A Remarkable Change Takes Place

I noticed the remarkable change in Michael's outlook and his state of mind. It was all for the better. I gradually felt able to read and digest the **National Bureau of Investigation Report** (NBI), which clearly clears Michael of charges made against him. This record goes on to a recommendation that Fr. Shay Cullen, Michael's Complainant, be deported on the grounds of him being and undesirable alien in the Philippines. (See report appendix 01)

Here is Michaels letter:

Dear David, July 3rd 2000

Just a few lines wishing every thing are OK With you and you are being to sort out how you will be able to see your daughter on mutual terms.

There is no movement with regards to my case with the Board of Pardon and Parole because as of today my prison records have not been sent from the prison document section to the Board. Every thing moves so slowly it really drives me crazy.

I am still reading a lot of Christian books. The one I am reading now is "Joy Unspeakable" by Dr. Martin Lloyd Jones. It is all about the Holy Spirit and I believe that baptism of the Holy Spirit is some thing distinct and does not always, as some people think happen automatically at conversion. The Holy Spirit is within every believer at conversion YES but the baptism can come at any time when Jesus Christ chooses to out pour it upon us. And if us Christian's are not aware of this and do not seek this ultimate experience I believe they are quenching the Holy Spirit, by not praying for it, and not just for them selves but for the whole Christian Church. "Revival".

Etc. Your are always in my prayers Michael.

News of Michael's Conversion

Michael wrote to me again to me in 2000 with news of his conversion to Christianity and of him being baptized, in a 45 gallon oil drum in New Bilibid Prison, by Lucas Dangatan, a former inmate, who was now a Religious Volunteer (RVO) working in New Bilibid Prison and Pastor of the New Bilibid Prison Theological Institute (NBPTI), in the prison.

I Finally Believe Michael

I finally believed Michael was telling the truth about his conviction. That he too had been "set up" for a crime he did not commit. This was clear to me after reading the National Bureau of Investigation (NBI) report, written by the Bureau in 1995. See Appendix **"Trojan Warriors"** to read the report. This report was brought to me by Suny Wilson, who himself had been wrongly convicted on a charge of rape. He called me on the telephone, on the 25th December 1999, soon after he returned to England, to introduce himself and he then came to see me with news of Michael and to give me the NBI report.

Michael Is Baptized In The Prison

As I was putting the final touches to the first edition of, **Converted on LSD Trip**, I felt compelled to include Michael's story (this is a STOP PRESS story) and must be told by Michael himself but in his letters to me when, I asked him to write his side of the story to compliment, "Converted on LSD Trip" he wrote in May 1999, "with regards to me writing my life story etc. For you to include in your book! Please David forgive me but I am so screwed up I just could not handle it right now it takes all my strength just to write this letter to you".

Our Church Writes To Michael

Our Church sent him a new leather bound bible and a couple of tapes and some friend wrote to him. He said also he was very pleased my fellow Christians were praying for him and were concerned about him. He expressed he was so very low and did believe in God and had asked forgiveness for all his sins and trusted in him. He wonders could any one ever love him and would he ever smile again or could he ever be happy again. Another reason why he could not think to write his story was because he said he was truly ashamed of many things I he had done and really did not wish to broadcast his evil past to every one at that time". He had confessed to the Lord and just hoped he would be forgiven.

In July 2000 Michael wrote he was reading Christian books and at that present time was reading, "Joy Unspeakable" by Dr Martin Lloyd -Jones. I was very encouraged and soon realized he had become a Christian when he expressed his wish to work in full time Christian ministry.

It became very apparent to me and to others that God had demonstrated His goodness to another undeserving sinner. Michael John Clarke. This was indeed good news to say the least. Armed with this good news and my intentions, I told my story to the religious correspondent at The News Portsmouth, Lizzy Miller.

THE NEWS Saturday August 12th 2000

ON THE left is Dave Clarke - college lecturer and committed Christian. On the right is his brother Michael - currently languishing in a prison cell in the Philippines.

Dave spends much of his spare time trying to help young people turn away from a life of crime. Now he is on his most important mission yet - trying to save his brother's soul.

Dave converted to Christianity almost 30 years ago, after sharing a life of crime with his brother in their youth. But his brother Michael went further off the rails and is now in a jail in the Philippines.

The New Article

The News Saturday, August 12, 2000

Dave, 52, of Hayling Close said, regular letters from his brother showed he was sick of his lifelong criminal past, and was thinking of becoming a Christian. He said: 'Michael wrote to me saying he was despairing and suicidal and asked me about my faith. 'I've been praying hard for him and believe he has now come to know the Lord as his personal saviour. I think he is listening to what I write.

Both brothers were notorious criminals in Buckinghamshire where they lived in the 1960's. They were jailed for malicious wounding, which involved shooting a woman in the face with an air weapon at Margate.

Dave said: "When I came out I knew everything there was to know about crime. It was a good school".

"I was determined to have the best of everything and went about it with determination. "I was riding on my brother's reputation. I thought he was cool, but others may not have done so. I set up a garage business for stolen cars.'

Dave went to Borstal for 12 months while his brother, who denied the charge, went to Maidstone prison for two years.

Father-of-five Dave went straight after converting to Christianity in 1970. He moved to Fareham where he began teaching electronics at the town's college, and became involved with the Christian Gospel Church.

His brother went on the run after being given home leave from prison but was recaptured and served his full sentence.

Michael is now four years into a 16-year jail sentence in prison in the Philippines for promoting child sex tourism. This crime he has always denied.

MICHAEL Clarke discovered the Philippines and its cheap sex business in 1995 when he set himself up as a tour operator.

He placed an advertisement under the name of Paradise Express in Exchange and Mart and produced crude brochure describing a 12-night holiday as the dirty dozen and with Photos of bikini clad women as well as giving details on how to find a Filipino wife.

Michael Clarke, who is divorced with a daughter, had been arrested: for agreeing that under age prostitutes could be procured, after he had been captured on a hidden camera. He is appealing against the conviction as an Irish priest set him up.

Dave said he hoped his brother would now find God and give up crime.

He added " I regret the hurt and pain I caused, but I realize I had to go through what I have because when I talk to kids to keep them out of trouble I have credibility.

Lizzy Miller The News 12th August 2001.

Our local news reporter Liz Miller of The News wrote to Michael, via e mail and asked the following questions " as follows:

Liz also wrote these questions for Michael on 28th Aug. 2000

Questions for Michael Clarke

1) How do you plan to get out of prison?

Answer - Conditional Pardon by way of voluntary deportation

2) How can we be sure you've changed your ways?

Answer - It is my Lord Jesus Christ that has convicted me of all my sins, but regards to the crime I was convicted for, which I will always maintain my innocence as Fr. Shay invented this crime.

Cullen who is an Irish Priest and he himself has been charged with Rape and a warrant is now out for his arrest with NO BAIL granted. The Victim is a 7-year-old girl.

Several foreigners have become victims of Fr. Cullen and The Modus Operandi of him is now under investigation by the Secretary of Justice whom hopefully in the long run will vindicate me completely from this present conviction.

The fact that I am now a true Christian and my FAITH will safe guard me from the temptations of the Devil. It is the same FAITH that assures me of eternal life. AMEN.

Michael tells his own testimony in our book **Trojan Warriors** that also contains the testimony of over 60 notorious criminals that had turned from crime to Christ.

I Publish My Book

It was a direct result of the news of Michael's conversion, from crime to Christ, that I felt compelled to finish my story. I had always, since my conversion, felt compelled to tell the world of what the lord had done for me. I had kept diary notes since the 16th January 1970 to do so. It was published under the title, **"Converted on LSD Trip"**, which was in fact the head line news of the Bucks Herald newspaper that told my story in 1971.

Cast Your Net The Other Side Of The Ship

I had a strong conviction that my story could be of great help to others and although I had tried to tell it in England a scriptural verse pressed hard on my mind it was, And he said unto them, **"Cast the net on the right side of the ship"**, **"And they were astonished, and all that were with him, at the draught of fishes which they had taken"**. Luke 5 verse 9.

The sense I gathered was that for years I had toiled to fish for men in my home country to win them for Christ and now I was to cast the net on the other side of the world rather than the ship to catch men for Christ. I shared this idea with the Church one Sunday and announced my intention to go and help Michael in the Philippines.

I had concluded that God in his wisdom had allowed all these things to happen to me and Michael, both the good and evil, to bring me to the point of testifying to the truth, of the goodness and mercy of God. It is my pleasure to do so. It is now as natural for me to glorify God as it is for a bird to sing.　　　　May 12th 1999.

Gordon Smith Contacts Me

My book Converted on LSD Trip had been published and a news article appeared in the Bucks Herald newspaper, in Aylesbury and as a result Gordon Smith, an old of Michael and contacted me and we renewed acquaintances. It was then we decided we would go together to the Philippines to assist my brother. It was decided we would visit for 3 weeks, as this was the longest time we could visit without a visa.

25 Our First Mission To The Philippines 2001

The Decision To Go

The decision to go and help my brother Michael was made in May 2001. Gordon and I went on our first mission to the Philippines taking with me 8 copies of my book, Converted On LSD Trip, to be given to The President of the Philippines herself, Gloria Macapagal Arroyo, The Director of New Bilibid Prison, Richardo Macala, The Director of New Bilibid Theological Institute Lucas P. Dangatan, and The Undersecretary of Justice Jose Calida. The City Mayor Olongapo City.

The full itinerary and record of the mission is tole in our book Trojan Warriors. We had a very successful mission in August 2001 through to October 2001. Gordon and I not only preached the gospel to many inmates in New Bilibid Prison but also in **Angeles City Jail, Barretto District Jail** and various churches in different parts of the Philippines.

Our Visit To Angeles City Jail (Click to view)

Trojan Warriors

Michael had worked hard with many inmates of New Bilibid Prison since his conversion . These men too had been converted from crime and worked together to help each other.

In August 2001, at one particular meeting within New Bilibid Prison, Michael and I had an idea (vision), which came to us simultaneously. We believed it would help and assist those inmates who had been converted, from crime to Christ, to write their testimonies and so we requested 100 men to write an account of their conversions. We promised to return the next year with their life stories printed in a book that we named there and then, **"Trojan Warriors"**.

It was purposed that each man upon their release would be able to take a copy of their book, with the accounts of the 100 men's conversions from Crime to Christ, as their own tool for evangelism. So upon their release they could go back to their own cities, towns of villages and tell of all what the lord had done for them and others.

It was this proposal that we worked together with Lucas Dangatan the whole of the next year to gather the hand written testimonies and put them together in our book, **Trojan Warriors**, that we were able to publish in September 2002.

Further proposals

We developed our ideas of helping inmates by the proposition of forming a Teacher Training College within the prison. This was to assist and help the work that was already ongoing amongst prisoners. Our idea was well received and **William C. Poloc** was one of the first inmates to be released and go home to his own city to preach the gospel in **Baguio City Jail**.

It was with this idea Gordon and I went to see the Undersecretary of Justice, **Jose Calida,** with proposal to allow men from our training college be released from the, **"Big House"** to go and teach the gospel within the Medium and Minimum compound prisons. Our proposal was met with great encouragement and it was suggested that due to the problems of security it was envisaged them prisoners from the Medium and Minimum Compound could be transferred to the Maximum Compound to partake in our teaching programs. We also spoke to Director of the Bureau of Corrections, **Ricardo Macala**, about our proposals and he agreed that with the support of the President herself this could be achieved.

The Same Gospel Truths

Michael and I had both experience the salvation of God and deliverance from sin and a life of crime by the saving knowledge of Jesus Christ. We knew the gospel was the power of God unto salvation to all who believe and felt constrained to teach these things to all we could and to help others to do the same.

In conference we had independently come to understand and believed the doctrines of grace which are referred to as Calvinism and we knew very few of those professing Christianity were in the dark and in fact some opposed these truths. This did not stop us working along side those who differed from us as we knew the truths of God are spiritual and a man needs to be taught by God these things in His own time. Jesus knew all truth and those he came to save were in the dark but that did not stop him coming along side and helping where he could.

End Of The Mission

Before leaving home for the UK one of or critics wrote a very complimentary account of our work which is listed below and I must say I felt good after such compliments. As the writer says we were just ordinary men doing what we felt we were called by God to do.

News Reports Of Our Mission

PRESS RELEASE

Reporter Alan Atkins. 11th September 2001

TROJAN HORSE MISSION TO THE PHILIPPINES

4th August- 10th September 2001

Preaching to prisoners including those on "Death Row", New Bilibid Prison, and Philippines. By Alan Atkins.

When first learning of the intended visit by self-styled evangelists and former Lecturer, David Clarke, from Fareham, Hampshire, and Gordon Smith from Merely, Nr. Bournemouth, England, to the Philippines, a number of resident foreigners were angry and dismayed. This was not for the fact that the pair wanted to share their experiences of conversion to Christianity that was their business. Rather, it was the deeper motive of purportedly attempting to assist in the early release of David Clark's brother, Michael Clarke, from the hell-hole that is called New Bilibid Prison, where he had been sentenced to serve 16 years. The angry resident foreigners, all of whom are involved in fighting to obtain justice for many foreigners falsely convicted in a country where the justice system is decidedly faulty to say the least, believed the visit would be detrimental to their own efforts.

Initially, the pair was to be accompanied by Albert Wilson, the Dover resident who had obtained acquittal and release from a death sentence just eighteen months previously. It was believed that certain local vigilante organizations, which had been screaming after his acquittal, would have drawn adverse publicity, which would have hampered the efforts of the locals.

German, Harry Joost, and Britain, Alan Atkins, had dispatched angry missives to David Clarke stating that they both could not see just what good the mission would achieve. Both believed that it would set the cases of incarcerated foreigner's back, as living here for many years, they fully understood the Philippine psyche. Vocal criticism by foreigners would lead to the Filipino authorities digging in their heels, just to show whose country it really was.

David Clarke, in particular, had a genuine reason to visit. There is little doubt that his brother, Michael Clark, convicted of running tours for paedophiles, was cleverly encouraged to make a silly, facetious remark while being secretly filmed by a British television company needing sensationalism. The case was gleefully seized upon by the self-styled "paedophile - busting priest", Father Shay Cullen. Cullen, who has a huge property overlooking Subic Bay, obtains millions from donations to support his children's home, which, incidentally, only contains between 26 and 36 children at any one time. Michael Clarke is only one of the high profile convictions he has obtained against alleged foreign pedophiles. Each conviction is accompanied by fan-fare overseas, mainly in Germany and Italy, and results in a massive inflow of cash.

David Clarke, learning some of this, had every right to visit the Philippines and assist his brother. Michael Clarke now claimed to have also been "re-born" being baptized in an oil drum in the prison yard. David Clarke, before arriving, did make one concession to local fears.

Discussions dissuaded Albert Wilson from visiting with him, so one problem was out of the way. David Clarke and Gordon Smith duly arrived and met with their Philippine hosts and coordinators, to begin a massive program of preaching not just in Bilibid prison, including to prisoners on Death Row, but also in various areas within reach of Manila, including the cities that used to host the huge U.S. bases, **Angeles City and Olongapo City**.

In these places, they not only preached in various non-conformist churches, but inside the jails. To the amazement of their local critics, they achieved an amazing success, especially in the prisons. **Literally hundred of prisoners** expressed that they wanted to learn more about the Gospel and themselves "be saved".

The religious will say this is a miracle. To the cynical, analysis tends to induce just how big a failure the Catholic Church has been in the Philippines. In the Philippines, well over 80 percent claim to be Catholic.

Indeed, most will have been baptized in a Catholic Church. Yet as over 54 percent drop out of school in primary, and even those who go to Mass will only listen to the homily, most of them know very little about Christianity. The fact that two very ordinary men, not wearing the "magic" vestments of priesthood, relate in simple terms, stories and the meaning of what is in the Bible, must have a huge impact. For the first time in their lives, they understand what being a Christian really means.

What makes it even better is that David Clarke readily confesses to them that 30 years previous, he was an incarcerated criminal, and that he discovered Jesus on an LSD trip. These men could, and did, relate to him. He was one of them, once. David's book, **"Converted on LSD Trip"** has just been published, which tells the whole story.

Critics Silenced

The critics have been silenced and instead applaud. Both David Clarke and Gordon Smith carried out their mission with dignity and respect for the Philippine people, and in fact, had proved to be a credit to the British people. Positive results have been achieved. They have suggested a scheme where prisoners can enter the ministry and preach in other prisons. This is under consideration. If their scheme is adopted and prevents recidivism, then their mission will indeed have been worthwhile.

Alan Atkins   11th September 2001

(Correspondent from Manila)

Trans World Radio

On my return from this first mission I was asked to relay an account of the mission work we was doing and again providentially this too was recorded. Here it is on Youtube

Converted On LSD Transworld Radio (click to listen)

A Joint Effort, We Worked Together

We worked the next year very closely with Michael, Lucas Dangatan, a former inmate and now Religious Volunteer, to write the book. It was published in September 2002 and in fact in the end 66 men submitted their testimonies which were all published. The book, by chance, was written with 365 pages, one page for every day of the year and 66 testimonies for every chapter of the bible.

In this book we outlined our proposals for a Teacher Training College that was to be run by prison inmates to help in the process of rehabilitation and reformation.

A copy of the book was given to each of the inmates on our return visit in October 2002. The Articles of Religion of our **Trojan Horse mission** were clearly stated and they were a transcript of the Bierton Strict and Particular Baptist Articles of Religion of which I remained a member by default.

William C. Poloc Sent to Baguio

William C. Poloc was our first Trojan Warrior to be released and his testimony is number 62 in our book, **Trojan Warriors**.

He was due for release in August 2002 and Michael and I commissioned him to return to his own City in Baguio and preach in the City Jail and Benguet Provincial Jail. He did very successfully.

We Fund William Poloc

We funded him with a monthly of Php 6600 per month, plus expenses and he did a very good job. He was commissioned to write a field manual for others to read as to how to take the gospel into the prisons of the Philippines. William did a very good job and went to Baguio City Jail and Benguet Provincial Jail and taught the gospel to may inmate and the ministry of Trojan Horse was recognized as a good work able to help in the rehabilitation of prisoners.

Again the doctrinal basis of William's work were Calvinistic or monergism as he calls it. These are in fact articles of religion of the Bierton Strict and Particular Baptist, 1831.

This meant we were all Calvinists holding to the truths of predestination, the sovereignty of God in terms of creation, providence and salvation.

William O. Poloc was released from New Bilibid Prison in August 2002, after serving 14 years. He was the first of what we hoped would be many inmates to be released. Trojan Horse planned to support financially many such men to do the self same work that we had commission William O. Poloc to do. This was the reason for the development of the Teacher Training College.

You can read Williams Poloc's testimony, which is number 62 in our book **Trojan Warriors.**

William O. Poloc Or First Trojan Warrior (Click to View)

26 Our Second Mission To The Philippines

Our second mission had taken one year to prepare and we took a team of 5 from England. Gordon Smith, Alastair Sutherland, Andy Macdonnell, Catherine Farr and Dr Richard Kent. On this mission we distributed our book to each prisoner that had written their testimony. Twenty Two of these were prisoners on **Death Row** and after our main meeting with the inmate we visited **William C. Poloc, in Baguio City,** or first Trojan Warrior to be released and go back to his own home to preach the gospel. This mission was thwart with difficulties and opposition.

Baguio City And Benguet Provincial Jails

We visited both Baguio City and Benguet Provincial Jail, in December 2002. William had worked continually in Baguio City and Benguet Provincial Jail and as a result of his successful work I had the privilege of baptizing 22 inmates in Baguio City Jail in December and further 8 souls in Benguet Provincial Jail, all of whom had become believers through the ministry of our sent man William O. Poloc. You may see the Youtube video relating to this

mission

Our Second Visit To Baguio City (Click To View)

Twenty Two Inmates Baptized In Baguio City Jail (Click to View)

William is committed and he continues to this day as an independent minister.

William Poloc our sent man at Benguet Provincial Jail

William Poloc Talking To The Warden

Benguet Provincial Jail

William Benguet Provincial jail

Michael and I Meet Together

In January 2003 Michael and met within the prison and summarized our plans and desires for the future as can be listened and viewed in the following Video on Youtube.

1 Trojan Warriors: The Beginnings

2 Trojan Warriors: The Vision

3 Trojan Warriors: Our Doctrinal Basis

These videos outline the beginning of our plans, the common vision and goal and our doctrinal basis for acting for which we learned later some men were opposed to us teaching these things.

27 A Revolt In New Bilibid Prison

Eat what is set before you asking no questions

Very early after we arrived on our second mission I was privilege to stay late in the prisoner and attend a function organized by a VIP inmate in the prison. It was a Saturday night and in Maximum Compound. This was a Privilege that was not opened to all RVO's.

There were many in attendance including inmate Commanders. Mayors and V.I.P's from Malacanang Palace. It was an exclusive Saturday night gathering of significant men in New Bilibid Prison.

This was not a religious group but men of the world. We were given food and drink and were accompanied by a **God Marshall Rescuer** as a bodyguard. (These men are specially appointed prison inmates- there are about 240 of them and they dress in black and are allowed to carry a wooden baton to show their sign of authority). These were not allowed in to the meeting but Michael and I were invited guests.

The next day it was reported that Michael and I were drinking wine (The Filipino "Born Again" Christians believed this to be a moral evil and was wrong) not only that but we were mixing with sinners.

This report spread quickly like wild fire throughout the prison. The fact was it was not wine but probably gin, which may have been made by the inmates. I learned later that it is in fact alcohol which was banned in the Prison. I have also since learned that inmates manufacture there own alcohol, in order not to be daunted by rules they do not respect. This drink is called **Tuba**. It seemed to me that these men did what they wanted an in fact actually run the prison.

Challenged

I was approached the next day by a lady RVO pastor called **"Cita"** who asked had I been drinking wine in the prison the night before. She seemed amazed that any one could do such a thing. I felt grieved in my spirit and realised that the spirit of those under law bewitched these people setting a bad example to unbelievers. They felt they should not touch or taste certain things like wine or taste certain things. I.e. These were of the opinion that righteousness was a matter of do's and don'ts rather than that of imputation of Christ's Righteouness. They did not seem to realize that it was not what the ear or drank that made a person unclean but rather the evil thoughts and gossip that came from within them defiled them.

They had fallen from grace or had never been freed from natural religion and they sought to bind others to their religious views.

Recollections of the Strict Baptists

Note. (I recalled my experience as a Strict and Particular Baptist minister in England in 1983) they were far stricter over many other issues than drinking wine.

One example was the Television. It was considered wrong to own a television set and watch such programmes as this was a means of defiling the mind and conscience and that we must keep our selves unspotted from the world. In their communities you were not allowed to own a television, because to watch such programs, brought the World into your home. So to them it was also a bad example to young believers who we desired to walking up rightly and not be conformed to this worlds standards.

To own or watch a television would be could be considered to be on par with a sinner, prostitute or atheist. They argued that if you use your liberty to watch the Television Set (even though you had a switch to switch it off) you could easily see things you should not be watching and be responsible to allowing your children and other weak believers to sin and stumble. So in order not to be a **stumbling block**, it was the Elders principle that no member of the Strict Baptist Church could have a Television set. If they did have one they would be put out of the Church Communion.

I recalled that these people allowed smoking and drinking wine but not the television Set.

It was as a result of this wrong censorship of someone else's conscience and liberty that I decided to publish my third book that is entitled "Touch not Taste not" or **The Bierton Crisis 1984**, in which I describe in detail my succession from the **Strict and Particular Baptist Church** situated in Bierton, Buckinghamshire England U.K. This I wrote in 1984 and had a limited circulation.

I now recall that it was exactly fourteen years to the day, after my call by grace, and conversion to Christ, on the 16th January 1970, that I withdrew from this Church as a matter of principle and conscience, which was the first and only church I had joined. This took place on 16th January 1984.

I seceded from the Bierton Strict and Particular Baptist Church because they had turned away from living and depending upon the grace of Christ to another Gospel. A so-called gospel of keeping

Law, traditions and customs of men. It was in fact the Law of Moses that they taught was a rule of life for the Believer and not the rule of Christ him self, which the Bible called the **"Perfect Law of Liberty"**. They maintained they kept the Law of Moses, including the Sabbath and did not watch the Television, or use an audio tape recorder to record sermons. All of this enabled them to keep them unspotted from the world, or so they thought. I was very concerned over all these issues and I was ashamed to be amongst them who should know better.

The whole of these issues I contended fought with for a long time period of time. This is the substance of **"The Bierton Crisis"**, 1984. I now realise why I was directed to write about it. I believe the publication of this book in the Philippines will help many and further the cause of Christ and His Gospel. It will be used to help many in the Philippines and elsewhere. The Bierton Crisis, **ISBN 9780953947348.**

Rejection By Sonlight Ministry

On November 23rd, 2002 , I went to New Bilibid (Medium Security Compound) Prison and Pastor Obispo Gani met me on the way and I informed him that I had the permissions from the Department Of Justice (D.O.J) to make the video of the inmates receiving their free bibles that were being given them by Gideon's International.

There were with him members of a group called **"Sonlight Ministry"** who were from the Maximum Security Compound and Pst. Obispo Gani was one of them. Gani was one of our Trojan Warriors and was our acting secretary and legal advisor, as he worked for the Department of Justice. They informed him they did not want to be associated with me.

I was surprised at this as the lady spokesman was the one we had asked **if she could** distribute our book **"Trojan Warriors"** to all our Warrior's at the Maximum Security Prison during the main event.

This group now did not wish to associate with me and decided not to allow me to go with them to give the bibles to inmates.

I was informed they were having a go at Gani for working with us. The reason apparently was that it had been reported that **I was a wine drinker and that we worked and mixed with notorious sinners in New Bilibid Prison,** and so I was not a true Christian like other more righteous people.

Gani said to me he was the Lord's free man and works where ever the Lord directed him (a good answer I thought) and so I soon realised how that Satan seeks to work in men to stop the good work of God being done. Gani suggested the problem was jealousy.

They said they were suspicious of our motives for making the video and were critical of our book Trojan Warriors.

They were in fact very dishonourable and I decided to bring the matter to the attention of their senior Pastor Dr. Tuico, who at that time was in America. He was one of the host pastors who had invited me to preach in New Bilibid Prison last year. I had met him and his wife and I was looking forward to see him on his return from the United States.

A Big Problem

Gani later shared with me in words which he describes as "a big problem", he said **"we have a big problem"**. He had received a text message from Dr. William O. Poloc who had been texted by an inmate at New Bilibid Prison reporting that Michael and I had gone to building 13 one evening recently and were drinking Tuba. That we were drunk and singing songs with two Bakla's (lady boys) late at night. That our conduct was known and our conduct was known to all the guards and all the inmates and was wrong.

I was told that the reason why members of Sunlight Ministries did not want me to video them giving away bibles was because I drank wine. They also were suspicious of us thinking we might put the video to misuse.

My answer to Gani was, "**I had no problem with drinking wine**". I accepted he and others might have. That I am not a drunkard and no one has ever seen me drunk. I confirmed that I did drink wine with sinners and others.

I also reminded Gani that I use to sell drugs, deal in sex and drank to excess before I was converted from crime and my sins to Christ on 16th January 1970. That my conversion was from sin, death and hell, in fact from crime to Christ.

I too stated to Gani that no one has come to me personally about this so called drinking or alleged misbehaviour except others who has acted on hear say. The gossip that had carried these stories were just the same as that spoken against the lord Jesus Christ in his day.

I accepted there was a concern for me as they felt that it was a bad example to prison inmates and not a Christian testimony. How ever that was their problem. Jesus drank wine and mixed with sinners and at night, so why think we should behave differently.

They said they did not want me to be rejected by the people who maintain drinking wine was a sin. They suggested I might be causing a **weaker brother to stumble**. One RVO went so far as to ask one of our team members (Trojan Horse International) not to smoke or drink at her home as it reflected on her, not because of it was unpleasant to her (she drank wine in private) but rather it was a bad testimony to unbelieving people.

My Question Is Who Is The Weaker Brother ?

My initial response was to ask whom have I caused to stumble as

I certainly was not aware of any one who had turned into a drunkard through me drinking wine with sinners any where. To the contrary I have spoken and encourage men to turn from strong drink to Christ.

I have no problem with what I have since learned with what they call "**Tuba**", except (My tongue in cheek reply) that I would encourage The Director of the Prison **Col. Ricardo Macala** to set up a manufacturing plant to produced bottled Tuba and legalize it. The prisoners could mass produce it and it could then be marketed abroad. I suggested that it could be as popular as Scots **Whiskey**. I may in fact be writing to suggest this to him and if he thinks it is a good idea he could write to the D.O.J. for such permissions.

Gossip Begins

Pst Obispoe Gani was then forced to leave Sonlight Ministries by Dr Oliver Tuico and due to his concerns about me drinking wine and mixing with sinners he withdrew from the Trojan Horse and joined Rev. Lucas P. Dangatan and the elders at NBPTI and the NBPCC group. It was then that the rumours began. It was reported that the Trojan Horse had 40 American sponsors and that we had received 4,000,000,00 dollars in donations.

In December 2002 I learned also that Lucas had not registered our ministry with the securities Exchange Commission in the Philippines. He had been given the money to do so months ago. So due to the trouble we were experiencing I asked Lucus to return the money that we had given him , which was in his bank account and was 1.1 Million Pesos.

Four days later we receive the petition from his men to get us out of the prison. He had instructed his men to write this petition to get us out of the prison.

It was also reported that Shay Cullen Michael's enemy had alerted the Catholic Church against our **book Trojan Warriors** and the Philippine Government had banned it.

It was also reported that I was a dishonourable visitor to the Philippines. That I had left my wife and daughter in England and was selling our family home because I had a girl friend in the Philippines.

They tried to ban us from the prison by denying our existence and they said we were not part of them.

It seemed that these men felt we were getting sponsored money but they were getting nothing. This was completely untrue as we had no money given to us from any one and Michael and I funded the whole mission from our private funds.

It so happened that the mount of money that was available for the mission was £40,000.00 and only Lucus was aware of the amount of money we had.

These men did not like our Calvinism and the fact we had spoken against women elders as they were being supported by women RVO's and they did not want to upset them. It was these RVO's who did not smoke, drink or mix with sinners late at night.

I call it Arminian righteousness and I call them the don't doers.

Gani had also spoken to a lady who had offered to renew my visa. She was given the money to do this but she did not do it. When Gani heard of this he suggested they contact the Bureau of Immigration and Detention and have me deported on the grounds of visa overstay. They were really against us and wanted us out of the prison.

None of them had seen the vision we were working too in seeking to bring help tom many of them and in assisting them in their declared intent to preach the gospel of Jesus Christ to men.

As a result of these evil reports word was sent back to England, from within NBPT/NBPCC, to my church, Gordon, Alastair and wife. These reports were believed and acted upon and no one asked me about any of these things except I got word that my sanity had been questioned by Gordon.

As a result of these evil reports emanating from the NBPCC, back to England, my Church withdrew moral support to me personally and Trojan Horse International Ministries.

28 First Petition against Trojan Horse

Get The Trojan Horse Out Of Here

Difficulties had arisen in the prison.

Michael and I had mistakenly believed these men in the prison would have the same desire as us to teach the gospel to all who they could. Michael and I had both experienced the power of God in delivering us from our criminal sinful past. We thought it would be a straight forward task to train and teach these men who had no religious traditions the gospel and how to share the true with others. We were mistaken.

This was because there were many religious volunteers who had gone into the prison before us and gathered groups of men together teaching their version of the gospel. I also realized what attracted most men was the amount of help in terms of food of goods that these religious volunteers gave them. Remember these men had no source of income and their food ration was 1 Kg of rice a day. There problem was that if they did not tow the line and follow the directive of their RVO they would not get their allowance. And if the RVO took exception to another group who they did not approve of then the prisoner would be discouraged from having any thing to do with that other group and if they did they would not benefit from that RVO's supply of goods. And if a particular RVO took exception to another person of group and disagreed with them then a word in the inmate ear would be sufficient to turn a nominal believer against them. I was personal informed by one lady RVO that one inmate had deceived her and gone so far as marry her in order to get support.

This happened in our case. There were many women RVO's who were called Pastors and they opposed the truth of predestination they were what I call the don't doers. They taught it was wrong to smoke, drink or sing secular songs. At the same time but they gossiped told lies about people behind their backs all which was really wrong.

This is what happen with us. I asked these elders, as part of their studies, to write an essay on the role of women in the church. Word came back to me that they would not do so as they did not wish to upset the lady RVO's who called them selves elders or pastors. Remember the scripture did not allow women to teach or usurp authority over a man in the church. These elders at NBPTI refused to write the essay as they did not want to upset there women RVO's. They also wanted me to stop teaching about God choosing men to salvation because their RVO's had taught them that they had free will

The Don't Doers.

The essence of the problem was that they had fallen into the trap of thinking and teaching they could please God by their don't do deeds. Do not smoke, do not drink wine, do not mix with sinners late at night, do not sing secular songs and so on.

A Denial of Imputed Righteouness

They seemed to be ignorant of the fact that the gospel taught that the righteous life of the lord Jesus Christ was imputed (reckoned to the account) of the believer and it was in that righteousness they stood perfect before God. They did not have to produce a righteouness in order to be accepted by God. This righteouness was a free gift, not earned and given to all who had been chosen to salvation. These believed if they denied themselves the thing they were forbidding they pleased God and it showed others they were good Christians. This was nonsense.

The bible says that the testimony they should have is a display of the love they have for others not gossip and back biting and speaking evil of others who were not like them.

On the 6th December 2003 I received notification of a petition regarding our Trojan Horse Mission. These men and elders had written to Rev. Lucas Dangatan about an incident that they were concerned about and had also sent a copy to the prison authorities.

Elders Responsible

Pst. Edwin B Tubiera	Pst Jose M. Franco	Pst. Ricardo C. Benitez
Pst Ricardo C. Bangcado	Pst. Salcedo A. Bagking	Pst. Hector R. Maqueda
Pst Tomas A Buchanilum	Pst. Anthony C. Dolin	Pst. Mel F. Nicolas
Pst. Cielito R Gan	Pst Basilo B Malarbob	Bro Domingo Lucag
Bro. Fatai Albi	Bro Pablo R Bebayle	Bro Enriquque A Yabanez
Bro. Efren C Roxas	Br. Arnel R Espina	Bro. Fausto V Manigding
Bro Domingo Alacids	Bro. Rufo Llenarisaz	Pst Adonis L Balad

Copy Furnished To: Supt. Office 1-OIC Office 1- File

Rev.Lucas P. Dangatan, Jr Pastor, Anthony Dolin. Assistant Pastor, Edwin D. Tubiera, Jose M. Franco, Richardo C. Benitez, Adonis L. Balad, Saledo A. Bagking, Hector R Maqueda, Jose C. Bangcado and **Elders:**

Effren C. Roxas, Arnel R. Espina, Domingo R Lucag.

The Essence Of The Complaint Was This

On the 15th December 2002, in the afternoon Michael and I met with the elders to hear the complaint, as they had convened a meeting to decide the future of **The Trojan Horse office** as it had been brought to their attention that Michael's attitude and behaviour, to some of them, had been unacceptable. He was irritable and awkward and ill mannered, which was contrary to certain rules.

Also it had been noted that Michael had been seen drinking Tuba and smoking in the prison and in our Trojan Horse Office. That a certain **Richard Gatwood** had been seen late at night in the office and Michael and he had a drinking spree with us. That when I left the office I was smelling of Tuba. This was their complaint and to them a bad thing. None of this had been checked out to see the truth of the matter.

Trojan Horse Office

Michael have built the Trojan Horse Office during our mission to the prison, on derelict land next to the bible institute study room, with the full permission of the owner Rev. Lucas P. Dangaton. It was used for all our mission work and housed all our equipment such as our video camera, television, printer and laptop computer. Michael also had permission to sleep there as a care taker and we use this for our ministry work.

It was later revealed that they were unhappy about Michael using the office as a dormitory they called it a Cabool and now it was not an office but Michael's room. They did not like this because no one else was allowed in our office it wasn't like an office they wanted i.e. That they could use it at anytime at all. It was stated that no one was allowed to use the schoolroom as his or her Cabool or as their own room so they **wanted rid of the Trojan Horse Office**.

They stated they did not know what we were doing in the office and they did not believe Michael. It was stated Michael was a liar.

The summery was that drinking Tuba and smoking was wrong and against the rules of their institution and they were concerned about Michael bringing disrepute upon them. They argued and said that Tuba drinking was not allowed in the prison and if caught it would lead to prison discipline. Any behaviour, which broke the prison rules would leave their Bible Institute open to questionable behaviour, which they did not want.

I Summarized My Response As Follows

I felt at first, on their first presentation of the problem, that there misgivings could be resolved but I was mistaken.

The issue about Richard Gatwood was a straight forward one as they had been miss informed by a gossip monger who slept in their school room and was their water carrier. Had they asked us about the matter I would have told them all about what happened but they never did.

Richard Gatwood was an inmate from London doing a 40 year sentence and had come to see me wanting help and I sought help him in what ever way I could. He had brought the Tuba and had a drink with Michael. I didn't like Tuba. When the guards came to fetch Richard Gatwood to take him back to his dormitory he tipped the tuba down the drain as it was against the prison rules. That was where the smell came from. Drinking Tuba was not immoral but distorting the truth and spreading gossip was.

I too had been disappointed with Michael's attitude and behaviour and had spoken to him about this during the second week of our Mission. The Team had also witness my opposition to him but they did not approve of me arguing with him over these issues in front of them, or others. That as a result I had sacked Michael from his position as Executive Director to his great disappointment and so I had dealt with the problem.

I was also unaware of the rules of their institution and prison rules. I was disappointed in Michael for not informing me or deliberately breaking the rules. That I had asked Pastor Andy to direct me to two good men who would spend time with me to share with me the values and ways of their culture- nothing had happened. I wanted to know about customs, which were different to the West and may affect the Bible Institute.

They Broke Prison Rules

I was aware that Tuba was not allowed in the prison and I knew of many rules that some of them did not keep such as possessing cellular phones and drinking whiskey or Gin secretly. Some drank Tuba. I stated that I had no problem in conscience over drinking Tuba or wine with sinners and I informed them that I was not a drunkard.

I stated that I did not smoke but could do so if I wanted too. I chose not to do so. My belief being that **the Kingdom of God is not about eating and drinking** but righteousness and joy in the Holy Ghost. That what one drank or eat did not make a man unclean but rather that the evil thoughts that came from the heart and spoken words that came out of his mouth defiled a man.

I stated that That I as a guest was very happy to keep the rules of the house this was the least I could do but stated I believed them to be wrong to expect me to stop drinking with sinners such as Bucla's (Girl Men) outside the prisoners in homes or bars or night clubs as I sought to preach the gospel to men in the entire world. I stated Jesus drank wine with sinners and so did I. That I was prepared to follow Christ.

It was stated that they expected Michael to stop smoking and drinking and sleeping in the office.

I knew also other people slept in the adjacent school room office so I asked for time to talk with Michael about this as he had been called away.

My Reply To The Elders Meeting

I wrote the following

To: The elders Christian Church NBP   19th December 2002

Further to my meeting on Sunday may I say that I now fully understand your position in seeking to secure the integrity of your institution. Michael and I fully support your endeavours. I was unaware of the problem that you had in Michael sleeping in out Trojan Horse Office. I understood that he was sleeping there as a matter of security, looking after all our equipment. I did not realize you had a policy that no one was allowed to sleep in and have a personal room at the NBP Institute..

In light of this problem and my knowledge of Michael, I have suggested to him that he seek alternative accommodation in the New Year. This will prevent further problems with NBPCC through any inappropriate behaviour on his part. Mean while he will abide by the rules of your Institution.

The Use Of Trojan Horse Office

It is proposed that the Trojan Horse Office be in continuous use by officers of Trojan Horse. That it be set apart for Trojan Horse International use. In practice this means myself and Pastor Lucas P.

Dangatan would share the office within its function continuing even after Michael's release.

That this office be used for Trojan Horse business, which will include:

Video productions, Counselling, Interviewing, Administration Business, Meetings, Teaching, Etc.

I would like to continue the developments, which we have already set in motion. I believe this will greatly increase the good work, which Rev. Lucas Dangatan has been responsible for in teaching the gospel and Training Teachers.

I would also like to add that I have offered my services to teach on a voluntary basis Theology and develop links at University levels in the United Kingdom and abroad.

Trust this meets with your approval and acceptance and we apologies for any undue harm.

David Clarke

Copy furnished to:

Andy Dolin

Lucas Dangatan

Michael Clarke

29 Second Petition against Trojan Horse

My Response Ignored

I felt my response to these inmate pastors was very reasonable and workable but it was just ignored. No one spoke to me or mentioned my response the them and instead a second petition was raise against us two weeks later, as can be seen below.

by NBPCC **directed by Lucas P Dangatan**

Dear Rev. Clarke

30th December 2002

We the undersigned Pastors-Teacher/Trainers are inmate-students from the different Churches inside this Compound, are withdrawing our unconditional support from the **"Trojan Horse Book"** for the following reasons to wit:

That we were not consulted and informed of the true objectives plans and purpose of the so-called **"Trojan Horse Ministries"**.

That **NBP Christian Church/NBP Theological Institute,** where the trainers and teachers belong, does not, in any way, directly or indirectly, connected with the Trojan Horse Ministries;

That the NBP Teachers Trainers school is none-existent and fictitious;

That **we were duped** into believing that the **Trojan Horse Warrior Book** would be solely compiled purely of our testimonies; but it appeared that there were some **irrelevant topics/materials** inserted/annexed therein;

That there is no truth to the allegation that the Trojan Horse Ministries is supporting the NBP Christian Church financially, spiritually or any other means;

That we came to know that the Trojan Horse Ministries is not registered with the Securities and Exchange Commission and even in England;

That the **self-imposed leaders** (brothers David & Michael Clarke) are persistently showing conduct un becoming of real Christian ministers.

That David Clarke could not fully perform his function as a minister because he has presently marital problems; and

That our membership with Trojan Horse Ministries is considered null and void ab initio.

Let copies of the document be furnished to proper authorities for their information.

List Of Inmates In Opposition

	Name	Group
1		
2	Anthony Dolin	NBPCC
3	Antinio Dolin	AGCMA
4	Antonio Satiquila	SMECC
5	Arnel Espina	NBPCC
6	Arnrdi Macalfe	AGMCC
7		
8	Art Pangillinan	SonLight
9	Basilio Malarbob	NBPCC
10	Blessie Valasco	AMCG
12	Bonifilo Martinez	SMECC
13	Celso Daluz	AGCC
14	Danny De La Cruz	AGCC
15	Danny Moreno	SMECC
16	Edwin Tubiera	NBPCC
17	Domingo Emroy	PWBM
18	Domingo Lucag	NBPCC
19	Eddie Sernadilla	AGCMI
20	Edison Quillantang	SMECC
21	Ernesto Ibias	AGCMI
22	Fernando Gujar	OMI
23	Garry Cave	NBPCC
24	Hector Maueda	NBPCC
25	Jeremy NestorDolosa	NBPCC
26	Jose Bangcada	NPCC
27	Jose Franco	NPBCC
28	Leonito Baquiran	JEMFM
29	Manuel Gano Jr.	NBPCC
30	Manuel Atadero	FJW
31	Marcial Llanto Jr.	CBFC/ NBPCC
32	Marion Lazaga	NBPCC
33	Moise Maspil	NBPCC
34	Nilo Ardon	NBPCC

35	Norberto Del Mundo		JFM FM BOC
36	Gogie Candelario		SMECC
37	Rolando Pagdayawan		SMECC
38	Romeo Ibay		BNPCC
39	Romeo Orio		SMECC
40	Rommel Deang		AGCMI
41	Rudy Hugo		SMECC
42	Ruro Llenarizas		PWBM
43	Sales Adic		SMECC
44	Sergio Jorolan		NBPCC
45	Tiddoro Laot		SMECC
46	Winnie Gacoyo		SMI
47	Jammie Jacobs		
48	Domingo Alacidis		NBPCC
59	Ricardo Benitez		
60	Aronis Balad		NBPCC
61	Mel Nicolas		NBPCC
62	Romeo Dianos		JFMFM
63	Ronald Labrador		JFMFM
64	Mario Biniahan		NBPCC
65	Salvador Baging		NBPCC
67	Cielito Gan		HNPCC
68	Ferninand Emocing		HNPCC
69	Efren Roxas		NBPCC

Copy Furnished To: Supt. Office 1-OIC Office 1- File

The Men Who Opposed Our Work

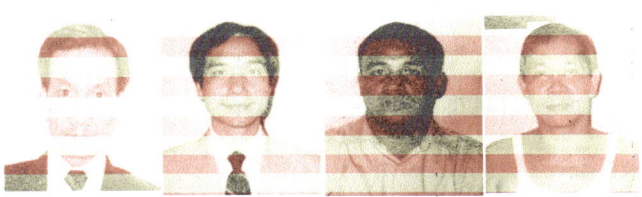

Lucus P. Dangatan   Anthony C. Dolan Jr.   Edwin D. Tubiera   Jose M. Franco   Richardo C. Benite

Hector Maruada   Jose Bangeda   Salido Bankin   Arnel Espina   Domingo luag

The principles upon which these men worked were not derived from the scripture but rather natural mans religion, the same morality of the Sadducees and Pharisees who condemned Jesus.

I call it **Arminian Righteouness** or the **Does and Don't religion.**

These men condemn smoking, drinking and singing secular songs and yet they will condemn a man with hearing him speak for himself, **back bit spread gossip and lie**, all of which he gospel of Christ condemns.

Leviticus 19, 18 You shall not take vengeance, nor bear any grudge against the children of your people, but you shall **love your neighbour as yourself**: I am the Lord.

These men give the gospel of Christ a bad name and they are said by some to be **Clingy Christians,** as they give Christianity a bad name. The principle being it is not that which goes into the mouth defile a man; but that which cometh out of the mouth, this defiles a man.

This people draw nigh unto me with their mouth, and honourer me with their lips; but their heart is far from me.

How I responded To This Petition

My first instinct was to ignore these matters as it seemed that it was a deliberate attempt to discredit and deny the work we had and were doing. All these accusations were based on gossip lies and untruths They were now denying all the work that had been done by myself Lucas Dangatan and others. **At least they acknowledged were not funding their institution and had any part of it.**

Who Funded Trojan Horse

The reality was we had funded the whole of the Trojan Horse Mission, Lucas and William Poloc's ministry. That Lucas Dangaton had handled over 1.5 Million Peso's of Trojan Horse International money that was used in visiting the many prisons and cities that we had gone too. It seemed these inmates and so called elders had no knowledge of these things **or were wilfully ignorant of them**. They were in fact denying the work that had been done

I was thankful that William O. Poloc was a living testimony to the truth and could confirm the work we had all done. We had fulfilled our promise of returning to the Philippines with the book **Trojan Warriors,** to give to each one of them that had written their testimony. They could use their book to tell of the great work that God was doing in the 66 mens lives that had testified to being converted from crime to Christ.

Our Evidence We Were A Ministry

The following outline of the Trojan Horse ministry was submitted at the request of the **Christian Mission Association** as part of the application for my full time Missionary and Visa Application.

Outline of Trojan Horse International (TULIP) Phils. Incorporated ministry

August 2001 to April 2003

Work commenced in August 2001 and:

1. Helped the New Bilibid Prisons Theological Institute with ministry, finance and encouragement.

2. Throughout the year from September 2001 to October 2002.

3. We assisted Rev. Lucas P. Dangatan and the teachers at the New Bilibid Teacher Training College with finance and continued support.

4. October 2002 to November 2003 we assisted 6 Philippine Pastors on Mission work in Angeles, Olongapo, Benguet Provincial, and Baguio City Jails.

5. Gave gifts of books printed in England and the Philippines to inmates and VIP's.

6. Supported local pastor of churches in Muntinlupa City and district.

7. Established an Incorporation that was S.E.C. registered as a none profit charitable organisation with Filipino members in March 2003.

8. Opened Local Bank Account with the Philippine National Bank.

9. We opened a Trade account with Globe Mobile Phone Philippines.

10. Formed affiliations with the National Director of the Values Formation Foundation Internationals Inc. (VFFII).

11. I was appointed a chaplain. Secured sponsorship from Apple Mac Computer Centre to assist Inmate Pastors in New Bilibid Prison in terms of 7 computers worth Php. 300.000.00.

12. Monetary Gifts and monies invested for the work of the ministry to date. All supplied by Trojan Horse International (TULIP) Phils. Incorporated,

Date	Amount PhP	To Whom And Purpose
1 August 2001	270,000.00	The Reformed Presbyterian Church of the Philippines to support and help the ministry of Director Joseph Kim.
2 August 2001	234,000.00	Laptop Computer
	108,000.00	Video Camera PAL
3 August 2001	3000.00	Electrical Meter. NBPTI Elders
4 September 2001	85,000.00	Pastor Castillo for a Lap top computer as a support for his ministry.
5 October 2001	14,400.00	Rev. Pastor Lucas P. Dangatan of New Bilibid Prison Theological Institute (NBPTI) for and assistance in the Prison and Pastoral work
6 January 2001	54,000.00	Pastor Lucas P. Dangatan support for Ministry work
7 October 2002	400,000.00	Pastor Lucas Mission work in Angeles City Baguio City, Benguet Provincial Jail
8 October 2002	225,000.00	Books as gifts for education to inmates and VIP's
9 August 2002 to January 2003	60,000.00	Pst. William Poloc of Baguio City for ministry work in Baguio and

		Benguet Jails and expenses
10 November 2002	11,000.00	Ministry Equipment
	28,000.00	Further Laptop Second Hand
	14,500.00	CD Burner
	50,000.00	Fire Wire CD Burner
	12,000.00	Laser Printer
	50,000.00	Video Camera, Video Tapes
11 February 2003	20,000.00	Apple Mac Computer to Pastor Ronaldo Lopez Muntinlupa City
12 February 2003	20,000.00	2X Apple Mac Computer Classic's
13 October 2003 to April 2003	84,000.00	Travel and expenses to local Ministers and assistance
14 August 2001	315,000.00	Books for Inmate and VIP's "Converted on LSD Trip"
15 July 2002	90,000.00	Transit Van (To be brought from England)
16 April 2002	144,000.00	Digital 16 Track Recorder.
	36,000.00	Drum Kit (To be brought from England)
17 April 2002		
18 August 2002		
19 September 2001	54,000.00	Computer 180 / 5400 (To be brought from England)
20 September 2001	108,000.00	Laptop G3
21 April 13 2003	9,900.00	Refrigerator
22 April 2003	63,000.00	Living Costs And assistance to pastors

Total Amount spent on ministry alone = Php. 2,562,800.00

Future Planned work

1. A second mission to Baguio City Jail in May 2003 with Philippines Pastors.

2. A mission to the Colonial Jail (Iwahig Palawan) with Philippines Pastors

3. A mission to the Kingdom in August 2003 with two Philippine Pastor to solicit funds for future work in the Philippines

4. Purchase property for office and residence for workers and inmates accommodation. Livelihood projects such as agricultural and appropriate needs that will assists the families. Export of Philippines products. Half way home and mission offices for outreach workers in their own City or town.

5. Promote Tourism to the Philippines from Europe for Christian minded people.

6. Promote work exchange programs for Government and private business.

7. The bring the Transit van, computers and equipment to the Philippines for mission work.

Prepared by:

David Clarke

Director of Trojan Horse International (TULIP) Phils. Incorporated

I did not need to defend myself from their misguided false statements misinformation and accusations. They had the responsibility to ascertain the truth about false accusations and not me. It was apparent they believed by denying the existence of The Trojan Horse they would benefit some how. I recalled that when Jesus went accused he did not defend himself against false accusations and was lead like a dumb sheep to his slaughter with out any protest.

Scripture Directive Ignored

The allegations made by these men were fabricated but mixed with some truth. The incident with Richard Gatwood was never looked into and so they never learned the truth about what happened

What they wrote was a fabrication and wrong. It was slander.

None could be substantiated by facts, as many points were just not true. In spite of my writing letters and reply's to all the petitioners the scripture directives, as to how to deal with such issues, were just ignored. As can be read in my book, **Before The Cock Crows, ISBN 9780953947331**.

All Trojan Warriors Had Withdrawn Their Support

In January, I learned from an e-mail, sent to me by my pastor from England, that all trojan warriors had withdrawn their support from our Ministry. This was the first I learned of this.

At the same time Gordon and Alastair announced their withdrawal from Trojan Horse, giving no reason for their withdrawal. This information was not true as not all Trojan warriors had with drawn as many were still with us including **Alfredo R. Nardo**, the Mayor of Death Row and other men on Death Row and William O. Poloc from Baguio.

I learned that lies and evil reports had been sent back to England about our ministry via certain people. Also rumours about my failed marriage had spread through out the prison. Gordon an Alastair failed to inform me of these developments and my Church did not ask me about any of the alleged difficulties that had happened during the mission.

My Pastor instructed me that I must subject my self to the eldership of Lucas and the NBPCC elders during my stay in the Philippines.

It was evident that he was completely ignorant of our work and the ministry we were involved in and accepted and acted on he evil reports sent to him from various sources. These sources were Pst. Obispo Gani, Gordon and Alastair. Lucas also was in communication with my wife and those in England.

As a result I was informed that my church had with drawn their support and refused to give me a letter of confirmation to say that

I had been a good Church member. I had requested this letter to support my application for a missionary visa in the Philippines. So can you imagine how I felt when I was let down. This letter was required by the Christian Missionary Association who had offered to help secure my full time missionary status visa in order for me to continue the work in the Philippines at minimum cost.

Silence Spoke loudly

I asked Lucas P. Dangatan to write and inform my Pastor the truth and reality of events as this was his responsibility as he was in constant communication with him and Gordon.

I Was Given Just Silent Treatment

The NBP Theological Institute was not a biblically constituted Church and not registered with SEC and so it was unreasonable and against the scripture for me to be subject to un authorised authority.

The members of NBPCC were all convicted criminals and it was unlawful for them to register any association with SEC until a period of six years had elapsed after their release from prison. All of these men were still in prison except Lucas and Pst Obispo Isagani. My pastor in England was just unaware of these things and so I felt forsaken.

I was an outcast

I was an evangelist and an Ambassador for Christ under authority to him, but **an outcast to these religious men**. As far as authority goes in connection with our Trojan Horse International ministry Lucas and the mission team were under my authority. This was because The Teacher Training College venture and Trojan Horse International were working together. I was the Director and Lucas the President. It was an organisation in reality and not fiction as these NBPCC elders were now saying. Gordon and Alastair had no authority and were no longer in Church membership in any church as the Lion of the tribe of Judah had ceased to exist before we left to the Philippines.

I had no recourse to speak to their co equal colleagues or elders in England. Pst. Obipo Isagani had trouble with his Pastor Tuico with who I was in correspondence and had left his ministry at Sonlight Ministries to Join Lucas in the NBPCC elders, in December 2002. Dr Tuico was not happy with Pst Obispo Isogani's conduct.

Conclusion

Men Pleasers Cannot Please God

It was my conclusion that men pleasers always think about what other people think of them.

Men Pleasers are like silly sheep they follow the crowd and not the Lord. They need a crowd to feel secure, this is because they have no confidence in the Lord to stand for truth and righteousness. They have the reward by the applause of men when they act to please the crowd.

My exhortation to such who know they are like this and have been men pleasers, is to seek God to give you a sense of His Awe and Might and His Holiness. Once you have seen the Lord, in His Glory, the **Fear of the Lord** will drive the **fear of man** away, like chaff, that the wind drives away, when the wheat is sifted.

My letter to Lucas P. Dangatan

January 20th 2003

Dear Lucas,

Re: Teacher Training College New Bilibid Prison

Further to the elders petition, and my request to you asking for your response and to send a letter to my church, along with an explanation to the elders of NBPCC. I am not sure as yet what your response is for you have not informed me. Gani has withdrawn, so has Gordon and Alastair.

William has informed me **he is with me in the Trojan Horse Mission to Baguio and La Trinidad**. I await the call to go and help baptise them. Are you going to come ?

I have with me all the written communications between us regarding the proposals and the development of The Teacher Training College, which you was in charge of from the beginning to this present day. These Elders have denied it's existence.

You sent me the details, photographs and status of the Teacher and Trainer and these have been published in Trojan Warriors

I have the details of the equipment we were considering purchasing, which includes a photocopier, to the tune of 65,000.00 Pesos.

It was you who wrote suggesting the change from a school to concept into a college, to which I agreed. And worked with you in it's promotion.

Further to this I in responded and took this on board. I took it very seriously and spent much time and effort representing our College at the highest possible levels, in the Philippines and to officials in Britain and the British Government.

Gordon and Alistair will confirm this if you ask them.

These representations were not fictitious, but based upon the proposals and ideas and realities that you informed me off and I accepted and promoted. Your we appointed as Our President by me.

You appointed Fernando Perez and others and I backed you in all you did. It was you who wrote to the office of the President and we received the reply regarding the opening of the **Trojan Horse Office in Laguna**. All of this was publicly known is known and was shared knowledge between myself, Gordon and Alistair and also Michael and many others.

William Poloc was the first inmate (Trojan Warrior) to graduate and be sent into the mission field according to our objectives as clearly stated and outlined in our publication, **Trojan Warriors**.

It would seem that either you did no inform your men at NBPTI, or the elders composing NBPCC, or some thing else has happened.

Do Not Call A Liar A Liar

Dr Hini says if I call a person a liar it is the highest insult so I will avoid using this term at the moment. Some one is not being honest some where. Some thing has happened. Please sort it out.

You are the one responsible to solve these evils as you are the President and Senior Pastor at NBPTI. **I actually feel you have a revolt on your hands** and the Elders have actually taken over from you.

Am I right? If so I can help you. Just call me as I am quite willing to take them all on. I have asked you to respond to me, in a Christian manor please do it for your sake. I am not on trial you are. You know what to do and I have asked you to do it.

Either way the Lord will honour his sent servants. It may be they are killed on duty. I am not ashamed to own my Lord and be counted with those who resist the Devil and stand for the truth and righteousness.

I wonder has Shay Cullen spoken to you or C.G.M. Regarding our book Trojan Warriors ? I have been informed that Pst Obispo Gani has informed you that the book has been rejected by the Catholic Church. If so you must tell me. Do not be taken in by such evil. I have been inform this may be the case.

I would like you to do as I ask. Please write to my Church and sort the problem out with NBPCC before I do.

Evil in New Bilibid Prison

I have witnessed great evil in New Bilibid Prison and I would value an explanation. I have seen a public live demonstration of a live chicken being ripped apart by its legs. This was by a Cebu dancer, before 1000's of inmates and visitors at New Bilibid Prison, on the Basket Ball Pitch. It seemed like this man was offering a sacrifice. He then bit into its side with his teeth. The poor chicken was alive and the man pulled out its intestines with his teeth, for the entire crowd to see. The Congress man was there, including the God Marshals. They all, or most looked in pleasure and gave applause. It did not seem to bother them.

What are you going to do about that ?

The chicken's intestines were pulled out of it's inside by the mans teeth. Intestines hung from the mans mouth and it's blood ran from his lips out of his mouth.

Fire-eaters and dancers in native costumes danced around the Catholic statue of St Nino. Giving praises to some thing or some one. What was that all about. I was shocked. This was idolatry.

This was awful. I witnessed one dear lady shocked and was horror stuck. When I went to comfort her. She reacted by vomiting when she saw it.

Why oh! Why!

Don't your men Petition about that ?

Why not revolt against such evil.

Are you children and not men and are gut less ? Where are the men of God, in New Bilibid NBPCC?

Why! Oh why? And who has bewitched you all!

You are taken up with issues of wine and smoking. You seek to take the speck of dust from out of a man's eye, yet you gulp down camels - your men gulp down 10 camels at once.

You Hypocrites

You let these things go and say nothing. You sing your songs and back bite and seek to defend your self's. You let such evils go on unchecked.

Why no protest from NBPCC Elders ?

I will be doing something about it. I have arranged to see Commander of the Cebu men to find out about this practice. Will you accompany me and assist me to make a representation on behalf of Christ? These men do this in the name of Christianity!!!!

I say unto you all, I am ashamed of you all. I say this in the name of my dear lord Jesus Christ and exhort you all to repentance.

Yes my view of Christianity is different to your Elders view. I love Christ. Who do they love?

Remember also I asked you to accompany me to preach the gospel to the tribal terrorist who beheaded the missionary last year. You said you would come with me when were on the way to Baguio to preach in Baguio City Jail. I hope you will keep your promise or shall I ask William to come.

Are you coming on the Baptism to La Trinidad at Benguet District Jail?

Yours in the name of our Lord Jesus Christ

Love David

Ambassador for Christ (Away from home, in a strange land).

Praise His name.

Baptisms in Baguio and Benguet

In January 2003 just after this revolt we went to Baguio and baptised 22 inmates in Baguio City Jail and 9 inmates in Benguet Provincial Jail, all the result of the work of William O. Poloc, or first sent man as a Trojan Warrior.

30 The Work Planted in Baguio Continues

William C. Poloc's Work In Baguio City

Thankfully our work in the Philippines was not in vain and we can report that our man William O. Poloc was our sent minister of **Trojan Horse International**. This I believe is confirmation, or the first indication that many such men will follow. I was called by the lord and sent by the Bierton Church and now my brother Michael had been called and we had now sent William O. Poloc on his mission that as we will show has been very fruitful. I believe this to be a vindication, by the lord, that I stood for the right things when at the Bierton Church in my contention for the cause of God and truth and also with those, in the Philippines, that turned from the way of grace, to follow the traditions of men.

I tell the truth in my defence and confirmation of the gospel of the Lord Jesus Christ. I believe we are living proof of the truth that all things work together for good to them that love God and are the called according to his purposes. Rom. 8 verse 28. That the things that have happened to me have turned out rather for the furtherance and confirmation of the gospel.

News from the Philippines

Re: News Up date confirming the ministry

Wednesday, 28 March, 2012 1:32 From: "William Poloc sr" <williampolocsr@yahoo.com> To: "David Clarke" nbpttc@yahoo.co.uk

To God be the glory!

We are all doing great anyway and my family as well. Regards to everyone. God bless!!

In Christ.

Dear David,

God's work here in the Northern Philippines bloomed most especially here in the city of Baguio.

The Baguio Christ-Centred Church also multiplied with the following daughter churches and other ministries.

We have:

2 The Pilot- Christ - Centred Church,

3 The Kamog Christ - Centred Church

4 The Christ - Centred Church Theological School (TULIP).

5 The Christ- Centred Radio Ministry, The Christ- Centred Jail Ministries etc.). We'll, we are truly blessed by these works He has entrusted to us.

Pastor's Day

Christ - Centred Ministries Philippines
Registration of Trojan Horse International

Due to the opposition that we experience from within New Bilibid Prison I felt it the right thing to do to register our ministry with the Securities Exchange Commission my self with the help of a Filipino Particular Baptist Pastor.

The Registration of Trojan Horse International

It was on the 16th January 2003 that I met a Particular Baptist pastor Ronaldo I. Lopez, at the Internet office in Muntinlupa City and we shared our experiences. He Stepped in and assisted me in many ways and for which I am very thankful to this day.

I noted the day, as this was exactly 23 years to the day of my conversion from crime to Christ. With Ronaldo's assistance I registered our Trojan Horse international (TULIP) Phils. Incorporation with the Securities Exchange in SEC Building, EDSA, Greenhill's, Mandaluyong City.

Our Security Exchange Registration Certificate

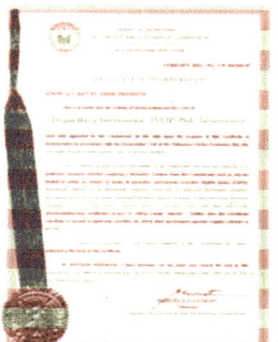

Trojan Horse International (TULIP) Phils. Incorporated

Registration Certificate

(The necessary proof of our existence in the Philippines).

Our Registration Certificate (Click to view our Articles of Incorporation)

Missionary Visa For the Philippines

The first thing I needed to do was to secure a full time visa permit to continue my stay in the Philippines and mission work to the Jails. In order to secure the necessary details I wrote to the Police in Fareham in the UK, Mr Ramsbottom, the pastor of Luton Bethel Gospel Standard Church, Mr Janes, one of our Trustees at the Bierton Church, Mr Crane our Church overseer from Lakenheath Strict Baptist Church and also Mr Peter Jacob an elder of the Portsmouth Gospel Church. This was in order to secure confirmation of my affidavit stating who I was and my credentials. I had present evidence to the Philippine Authorities of my legitimate credentials.

Sadly but thankfully I received some help from the UK. Mr Ramsbottom replied to my request and so did and also Mr Janes but the sad thing was Mr Janes, one of our trustees of the Bierton Church, did not tell of the closure of our Bierton Chapel. Also Mr Peter Jacob due to the bad reports, which were spread in the UK about our work in the Philippines, refused to help in any way and would not confirm that I had attended their meetings and had been in good standing. I felt so alone and let down. I recalled at that time that it was this man, along with one of his elders and a so called lady Reverend that who opposed the first publication of my book **Converted on LSD Trip**.

I am sure the Apostle Paul felt forsaken, as I did when he wrote, For Demas hath forsaken me, having loved this present world. 2 Tim 4 verses 10.

Help from the Chief Chaplain

The appointed Chief Chaplain for the Philippine Prison Ministries Rev. Monico Carany assisted me and with his direction and assistance of the **Christian Missionary Services** at Pasay City, I had to undergo medical and psychological examinations including X-rays, HIV tests and intelligence tests, and as a result I was cleared and accepted and had a Psychological Report. I was thankful for this as I had herd from the UK my mental health had been called into question.

Medical And Psychological Examination

Date of examination 2nd April 2003.

Interpretation Of findings

The subject possesses an average intellectual functioning and is able to express his thoughts and views. Has been noted to be responsive and open to social contacts. Observed to be work orientated and has a very positive outlook in life.

Emotionally, the subject manifests slight insecurities and loss. Evasive tendencies are relatively minimal.

Remarks:

Recommended.

My application was accepted and my admission status from a temporary visit under Section 9 (a) to Quota Immigrant Visa under Section 13 of the Philippines Immigration Act of 1940, as amended in my favour and granted to Rev. David Clarke a British National on the 10th April 2003.

It cost us in excess of Php 100,000.00 (£1000 GBP) to gather together and pay for all the required tests, examinations and documentation. The result was that I could permanently work, according to our Articles of Incorporation throughout the Philippines, as a missionary and return to the UK for two months of the year before having to return. It was some comfort to learn the results of this examination as I had heard that my sanity had been called into question and it had been rumoured that I was ill.

I had Incensed Religious Carnal Men

The truth of the matter was I had incensed the religious carnal mind, in certain religious men, who were then moved by another set of principle other than that the gospel of our Lord Jesus Christ. I was thankful for the scripture record that told me this was a normal reaction from ungodly men. Then answered the Jews, and said unto him, Say we not well that thou art a Samaritan, and hast a devil? Jesus answered, I have not a devil; but I honour my Father, and ye do dishonour me. John 8 48-49.

Working Within New Bilibid Prison

It became necessary to begin our work again within New Bilibid Prison and so to this end we appointed Gonzales Arnel Perpiton Bautust as our Religious Volunteer (RVO) and he worked with twelve inmate within the prison.

Religious Volunteer Appointments

My Status was established as an Extraordinary Religious volunteer which brought with is certain privileges to work with in the prison

We Buy Land Within The Prison

We were able to purchase a small lot of land within the prison and Arnel worked with the prisoners and built a function room to conduct meetings. (Not that this was possible as all property belongs to BUCOR, but inmates can claim ownership by continued use of land for what ever purpose).

Our RVO Arnel	David Clarke RVO

My RVO Identification for New Bilibid Prison

Funding Of The Mission

I don't' wish to really talk about money as the Lord provided funds for his work in His own way. How ever because evil men and people who pry into other peoples business, and also to silence the gainsayers, for the record both Michael and I provided all the funds from our personal resources. And between September 2000 and May 2005 we provided all the funds for the mission work, to the tune of £50,000.00. English pounds and on Michael's death he left £10,000.00 to his daughter.

We received no funds from anywhere else except a gift from the Christian Gospel Church, of £400 in July 2001. Our Trojan Horse funds supplied all the return airfares for all our 4-team members, all their accommodation expenses and travel arrangements for the 2002. The Trojan Horse mission was paid for by Michael and I. We had no funds from anywhere else and we did not seek sponsorship. The accounts for our Trojan Horse are available upon request.

31 Michael's Death and Burial

Michael sadly died in New Bilibid Prison before our vision of bring help and release to many had materialized, on the 27th May 2005 and was buried in **Olongapo City** cemetery by Harry Joost, from Baloy Beach and we held a memorial service of celebration regarding his life, death and conversion, from crime to Christ at our Bierton Baptist Chapel.

Michael Exhorting Men On Death Row

Michael preaching on Death Row in New Bilibid Prison

I had always considered Michael as a member of our church at Bierton when he was baptized according to my instructions, in the Philippines. I had received him and others too as a Christian and was considered to be a member of the body of Christ. And so in my continuos role as the Director of Trojan Horse International (TULIP) Phils. Incorporated I conducted a memorial and thanks giving service for Michael at our Bierton Chapel Cemetery. Friends were invited, including Dave Courtney and Malcolm Kirkham. For their own reasons they did not attend the memorial meeting Malcolm Kirkham did attend an audience with Dave Courtney at the Britannia pub that evening. A meeting that I had arranged for us that evening.

In the above picture we see Michael speaking to men on Death Row giving them words of encouragement and consolation as their hope was to be in the lord not man.

Further Good

Malcolm Kirkham as I have already written about and my friend in early years has read my book and listed to my story and he too at the end of his life has confirmed that he too turned around from his life of crime as a direct result of my influence. It is my hope too the Dave Courtney does the same.

Our memorial service at our Bierton April 2005

Michael's Tomb Stone Bierton Chapel

Bierton Chapel Cemetery

Several men from New Bilibid prison have been released and gone home to their own cities to preach the gospel. They are former drug dealers, killers and real criminals. William C. Poloc is just the first fruits of the harvest. You may read their testimonies in our book **Trojan Warriors**. Or you my write to William C. Poloc to get updates and news of their work. This would encourage them.

Michael In His Coffin

Michael Asleep

Michael Tomb Stone Or Plaque Of Remembrance

He Being Dead Yet Speaketh
The Good That Has Come

32 Essence Of My Learning

I am able to conclude from my own learning and experience that there are certain truths taught in the bible which are fundamental to effect a change of life in a person.

The first of these things are:

1 To accept the reliability of the bible

2 To accept the truth that bible tells of the origins of man the purpose for our existence.

3 That we are accountability to God

4 To accept the bible that tells of judgment for the way we live and act toward each other selves.

5 To believe that God does forgives sins

6 To accept what the bible says as to who the lord Jesus Christ is.

7 To receive the truth that Christ died to pay the debt of man's sins

8 To believe that if we believe the truth and turn from our wrong ways then all our sins, past present and future are forgive.

9 To accept that every one who believes the gospel (good news) are the children of God. It does not matter what your past has been.

10 To accept that a person who receives Jesus Christ becomes a new man and all his past wrong is wiped out and a new life begins.

11   Understand the doctrines of grace.

There are many more things but sufficient to know that all of these things are expressed in theological terms and may be further examined by considering the follow subject matters that I treat in my other books, **Bierton Strict and Particular Baptists, The Fall Desperation and Recovery, Trojan Warriors** and **Mission To the Philippines.**

The main issues are:

1. The Sovereignty of God
2. The Doctrines of Grace
3. The Infallibility of Scripture and the relative Accuracy of the Authorised Version of the bible.
4. The Deity of the Lord Jesus Christ
5. The new birth
6. Predestination
7. Articles of Religion
8. Drinking wine, Mixing with Sinners, Worldliness, Sabbath Days
9. Eschatology
10. Head coverings
11. Hymn Singing
12. Singing secular songs
13. Baptism or baptisms
14. Women elders

All of which need to be address by those who are teaching the Christian Religion.

33 My Return to The UK

Due to the very remarkable opposition and learning experience we had in the Philippines I realised the way forward is to educate people in the same way that Michael and I had done. This would give them a grounding in truth and religion and help them in their own way of reformation and rehabilitation.

It is our belief and vision that a similar work and help in the process of reformation and rehabilitation can be accomplished in our prisons in the UK.

Punk Rock Opera

On my return to the U.K. and after my second mission to the Philippines in 2004 I found very few people found the time to read books and so I decided to put my story of Converted on LSD to a Punk Rock Opera called Borstal Boy. This was discussed with **Mick Fisher** one of my former students at Fareham college who was the leader of the band **The Asylum Seekers,** from Gosport. It was soon agreed we would use their existing punk rock classics to tell the story.

Positive Responses From British Prisons

A draft copy of **Converted on LSD** was sent to over 30 prison chaplains in the UK, Including **HMP Belmarsh, Manchester, Risely, Lindsholme, Parkhurst, Erlstoke, Feltham and Hull** and as a result almost 500 copies was requested for prison inmates. As a result a special edition has been produced called **Borstal Boys** that addresses some of the criticisms that were received about the draft edition sent to prison chaplains. Two hundred and fifty copies are being sent to inmate in 40 prisons before December 25th 2013.

This punk rock opera, **Borstal Boy,** has been designed to be performed in British prisons and other public venues.

It is believed that the gospel is the power of God unto salvation to those who believe and God has not chosen many wise or noble men but rather the weak, despised the castaways, even prisoners and criminals, to work reformation in their lives. It is believed this unique way will get the story of reformation to people who would not otherwise hear it.

The Book

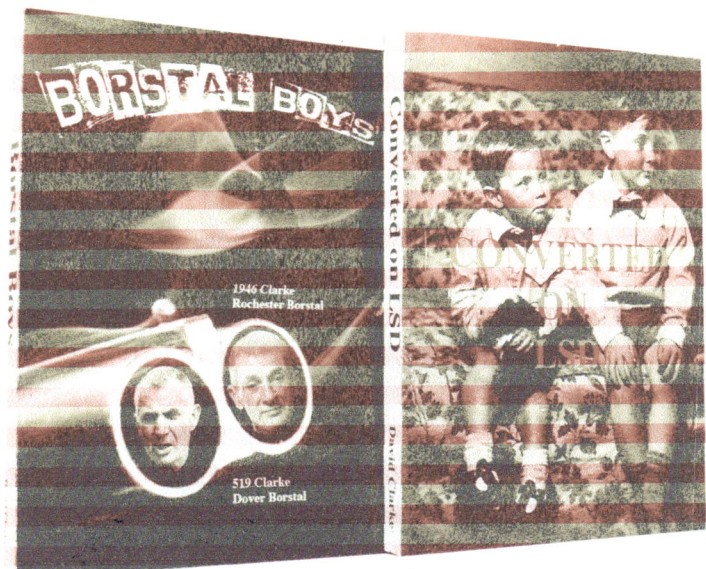

Alternatively Borstal Boys   Converted On LSD

Winchester Prison

With the help of Caroline Dinenage, MP for Gosport, Mark Hoban, MP for Fareham and Steve Brine, MP for Winchester we have approached the governor of **HMP Winchester Prison**, David Rogers, who directed us to Gary Wright, the Head of Re-offending Prevention, to consider our proposal to perform our opera that is called **Borstal Boy** for the benefit of prison inmates, with a view to encourage them to read our story as published on a special edition of my original book **Converted on LSD**.

We have also had requests by two prison chaplains for the opera to be played in other prisons and we intend to do so.

I am available to share my story with prison inmates and help in what ever way I can and the band are also available to perform our punk rock opera Borstal Boy in any prison place or venue.

Stop Press

The Asylum Seekers are booked to perform our opera at The kings Theatre, Portsmouth, Saturday 26th April 2014

The Kings Theatre Portsmouth

Our Advertisement In The King's Theatre Brochure

31 Other Publications

1. Converted LSD Trip 2nd Edition
   ISBN: 0953947355
2. Trojan Warriors
   ISBN 0953947319
3. Before the Cock Crows
   ISBN: 0953947335
   This tells of the trials and difficulties that we experienced during Mission to the Philippines.
4. The Bierton Crisis
   ISBN 0953947348
   David's Secession: From the Bierton Strict and Particular Baptist Church in 1984. This was David's the first Book

   Audio and Video Recordings (Click to view)
5. My Testimony Audio recording:
   David's Testimony made at Luton on, 22nd March 1972
6. Fishing for Men: Video
   Preaching at Bierton June 5th 1983
   The Bierton Meeting.
7. Michael Clarke's Testimony
   from New Bilibid Prison, Philippines

8 Mary, Mary Quite Contrary
   "Does the Lord Jesus want women ruling His Church?" David secession from the Jesus is Lord Church at Warsash, 1999

9 Bierton Strict and Particular Baptists
   ISBN 0953947379. This is the continuing story of Converted on LSD

10. Converted on LSD Trip video Playlist